You're the end of the rainbow, my pot of gold ❧ You're daddy's little girl

You're the spirit of Christmas, my star on the tree ❧ You're the Easter Bunny for mommy and me ❧

to have and to hold ❧ A precious gem is what you are ❧ You're mommy's bright and shining star ❧

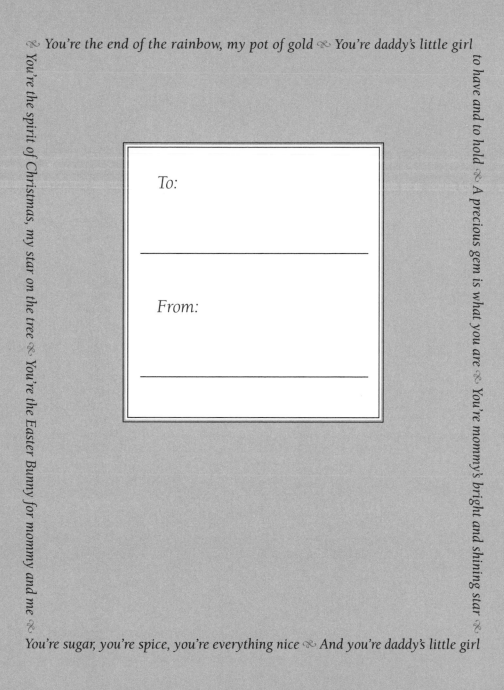

To:

_____

From:

_____

You're sugar, you're spice, you're everything nice ❧ And you're daddy's little girl

*Tape a photo of you
and your loved one here*

Daddy's Little Girl

Daddy's Little Girl

Stories of the Special Bond Between Fathers and Daughters

GREGORY E. LANG

HarperOne
An Imprint of HarperCollinsPublishers

HarperOne

HarperCollins books may be purchased for educational, business, or sales promotional use. For information please write: Special Markets Department, HarperCollins Publishers, 10 East 53rd Street, New York, NY 10022.

HarperCollins Web site: http://www.harpercollins.com

HarperCollins®, ■®, and HarperOne™ are trademarks of HarperCollins Publishers.

FIRST EDITION

Photos: Courtesy of Gregory E. Lang.

LIBRARY OF CONGRESS CATALOGING-IN-PUBLICATION DATA
Lang, Gregory E.
  Daddy's little girl : stories of the special bond between fathers and daughters / Gregory E. Lang. — 1st ed.
       p. cm.
   1. Fathers and daughters—Anecdotes. 2. Fatherhood—Anecdotes. 3. Parenting—Anecdotes. 4. Adult children—Family relationships. I. Title.
  HQ755.85.L336 2008
  306.874'2cdc22   2007044768
         ISBN: 978–006–145149–2

08 09 10 11 12 RRD(H) 10 9 8 7 6 5 4 3 2 1

TO MY LITTLE GIRLS,

Bug Meat and Monkey Feet

Train a child the way she should go,
and when she is old she will not turn from it.

PROVERBS 22:6

∿ INTRODUCTION ∾

ONE DAY WHILE at work, I had a conversation about my relationship with my then eight-year-old daughter, Meagan, my only child. A divorced dad with joint-custody privileges, I had Meagan for two weeks each month. This on-again, off-again visitation schedule at times created challenges for me, both at work and in my personal life. Yet, it also gave me a wonderful opportunity to be involved in my daughter's day-to-day activities. I organized my schedule around hers during our time together, skipping lunch in order to leave work early enough to pick her up from school and hosting slumber parties on our weekends together.

During that workplace conversation, I was asked if I truly enjoyed the rewards of parenting, or if they were overshadowed by the challenges I faced as a single dad raising a young daughter. I answered quickly and adamantly—the rewards were endless and worth any challenge or lost opportunity I had to deal with. For the remainder of that afternoon, my thoughts were filled with one reason after another about why I would rather, and without hesitation, compromise my career and single lifestyle than my relationship with my beloved little girl.

A lifelong note taker and list maker, I sat down when I arrived home that evening and in short order wrote out a list of reasons why I thought Meagan needed me—indeed, why I needed her. I ended up with one hundred reasons.

That list was originally like so many others I had written before, an attempt to get thoughts on paper before they were forgotten. When I finished the list, I read it over—once, twice, and then many times. At some point, I saw my written words as more than a simple list—they were a tribute to

1

our relationship, a reassurance to my child that her father will always love her, passionately and unconditionally, no matter what.

It was also, quite frankly, a tangible reminder of what I, as one of her parents, should do for her as well as what I hoped not to ever do.

When it occurred to me that I had read the list over a dozen times before putting it down, the idea for my first book was born.

Nearly four years later, the book was published; it was titled *Why a Daughter Needs a Dad: A Hundred Reasons*. I still remember the day Meagan and I first spotted copies of it on a bookstore shelf. My own words, on bound paper and in hardback no less, were right there in front of me! Even if no one other than my family and friends were to buy the book, I was proud of it. And it influenced our relationship in ways I had not expected.

We began to talk more often about our relationship and improve upon it where we could. I worked harder to live up to my published words, and she began to have a better understanding of what concerned and motivated me as her father. A few times, she even reminded me of what I had written when I was not conducting myself or handling a matter as I had suggested I should.

Soon, we learned the book connected with others as well. I began to receive letters and e-mails from dads and daughters from all walks of life who wanted to tell me about their relationships. Many were from daughters who heaped praise on their dads; others were from dads who told of their hopes and dreams for their daughters. Occasionally, a daughter wrote to express her longing for a dad who had passed away, and now and then a perplexed or frustrated dad would ask for advice. Most messages from daughters included hints of what a dad had actually done, knowingly or not, that contributed to the happiness and well-being of his loving daughter.

Today when I ponder my relationship with Meagan and now also with my stepdaughter, Linley, wondering how best to handle or think about this or that situation, I often turn to my cache of e-mails and letters. I scan them for advice and reassurance; surely some other dad has told me of when he was in a similar predicament, or a daughter has inadvertently described for me what to do when I find myself in a certain father-daughter quandary. Thankfully, I always find at least one note filled with welcome wisdom.

It occurred to me on one occasion while reading these stories that perhaps with the advice and insight I've found in them, I could help other dads and daughters better understand their own father-daughter relationships. With that idea in mind, the plans for this book began to materialize.

I corresponded with my readers, asking them to elaborate on stories they had shared with me and to tell me new ones. I wanted to hear what dads and daughters had learned from each other, how their relationships had changed over time, what challenges they faced and how they dealt with them, and what their favorite memories and special moments were.

I eventually received nearly four hundred stories—stories that not only continued to teach me a thing or two, but also reassured me there are plenty of dads and daughters who want to celebrate their relationships by sharing them with an eager and appreciative audience. I received funny and heart-warming stories about birthdays, daddy-daughter dates, emergency-room visits, graduations, weddings, late-night chats in the dark, and so much more.

As I read the stories, I began to notice a few common threads running through them: Fathers and daughters have a tremendous capacity to love each other no matter how challenged their relationship might have been at one time or another. And no father ever thinks his daughter is too old to call on him for help of any kind, just as every daughter eventually realizes she, no matter what her age, will always be her daddy's little girl.

That brings me to the little girls in my life today. Meagan is now a high-school senior preparing to enter college, and nearly every day we are reminded that in just over a year she will not only leave home but our community as well. For her, this book is a reflection on the times we've spent together since I wrote *Why a Daughter Needs a Dad* and a reminder that though she may leave the nest, she can never leave my heart. My step-daughter, Linley, has now lived nearly three years with me and is embracing a new kind of daddy-daughter relationship, one with a stepdad. For her, this book is a promise that she can have as much of me as she wants, and in these stories I hope she sees just how much that can be.

You are about to read stories about dad-and-daughter relationships, some downright funny and obvious, others subtle yet thought provoking. Dads, I hope you will finish this book with the same feelings of enlightenment and inspiration I experienced while writing it. And, daughters, after you've turned the last page, I hope you give your dad a great big hug and a kiss. I assure you, he'll be delighted that you did.

﹏: AUTHOR'S NOTE :﹏

This book is a collection of stories about fathers and daughters. Simply put, I could not have written it without the generous permission of daughters and dads to tell their personal and heartwarming stories alongside my own. In addition to permission, they also granted me editorial privilege to retell their stories as I saw necessary for the sake of creating an even book that would be enjoyable for all to read.

Stories were sent to me by traditional mail and e-mail and through my Web site or were told to me in recorded face-to-face and telephone interviews. As you might guess, the writing and storytelling styles I encountered varied considerably. In some cases, English was not the primary language of my source, making editorial changes all the more essential to create a brief but readable story for my audience.

In every case, however, I stayed true to the original daughter-dad story, even sending many of them to the storyteller for review and input. I hope that those who read their own stories in the following pages will be satisfied with how they were reproduced in my voice and then woven together with other positive messages about daughter-dad relationships.

I photographed family and friends to illustrate this book. No relationship between the models and the stories is implied by the placement of a photograph before or after a particular story. Finally, real names were not used in this book in order to respect the privacy of all the persons portrayed within each story.

Gregory

Daddy's Little Girl

❧ THE CENTER OF HIS WORLD ❧

MARGO'S HOUSE FINALLY sold after being on the market nearly three years. She and her husband were so happy to finally have a buyer that they signed a contract requiring the family to move out within two weeks. Despite the inconvenience, everyone pitched in to prepare for the expedited move. Then, two days later, Margo's mother-in-law died suddenly and unexpectedly.

Although she tried to plan a funeral and continued to pack up their home, Margo accomplished little, her progress constantly disrupted by her tears of grief and overwhelming worry for her distraught husband.

Concerned about his daughter's situation, Margo's father told her not to worry about finding a new place to live and that she needed to grieve and be available to support her husband. He suggested she and her family of four move back home with him and her mother, at least until the dust cleared.

Even though her parents' company and accommodations provided Margo with much-needed support, she still needed to fill the void left by her mother-in-law's death. The two women had been close, and Margo felt the pain of her loss almost as intensely as her husband did. Soon, she found herself going to her parents' mailbox every day, hoping for mail—a card or handwritten note from a friend—something to make her feel better, lift her spirits.

One day, disappointed once more after not finding any mail addressed to her but seeing stacks of it in the box for others in the family, she expressed her doubts about being important to anyone.

Her dad overheard the comment.

The next morning when Margo entered the bathroom, she found handwritten notes taped to the mirror. She also found notes in every drawer in her bedroom, in the kitchen cabinets, nearly everywhere she looked. On the notes were messages that said, "Someone loves you," "Someone's thinking about you," and "You matter to me."

They had all been written by her dad. Her heart began to lift, and she smiled again as she peeked here and there, searching for other notes of love and solace.

Several days after finding the hidden notes from her father, Margo made another trip to the mailbox and discovered a letter, this one addressed to her. It was from her father. He had written it at his office just four blocks away and sent it through the mail so she could find a letter to her in the mailbox. Opening it there on the sidewalk as tears ran down her cheeks, she read of the kind of love only a father can express to his cherished daughter.

Her dad continued writing and mailing letters to Margo for more than a year, telling her how much he loved her and what a wonderful daughter, wife, and mother she was.

During that time, Margo's grief fell away, and, of course, she realized just how important she was to someone special—her dad.

"He is not only my dad,
but my best friend and confidant, too."

❦SPECIAL MOMENTS❧

DICK ENJOYS SPENDING his days of retirement in Florida, sitting in the sun and reflecting on his long life and list of accomplishments. At the top of his list is the knowledge he has raised two wonderful daughters; his little girls have become grown women he can be extremely proud of.

Inevitably, whether when looking at old photographs or daydreaming about memorable events in his life, his thoughts turn to the days of four decades ago, when his little girls looked up at him with dancing eyes and thought he was the source of all things fun and joyful.

One morning, as images of Evelyn, his younger child, played like a treasured home movie in his imagination, a song suddenly popped into his head. It was a song he had not thought of for many years, and although he could hardly remember the last time he had sung it, every word came to him as if it were just yesterday that he had memorized it. He sat down at his computer and quickly typed an e-mail to his forty-six-year-old daughter, one that included a few lines from that song:

> You're the end of the rainbow, my pot of gold,
> You're daddy's little girl to have and to hold.

Moments later he received an e-mail; it was from Evelyn. She was crying at her desk, she told him. She hadn't heard that song in thirty-five years. It had been her favorite bedtime song, one that Dick always sang to her each night while he made sure she was warm and snug beneath her bedcovers.

Even though Eveyln is a grown woman, hearing her dad say that she is still his little girl touched her heart that morning just as it had each night when she was a young girl. She went on with her day, knowing that no matter what challenges they may have faced over the years or how many miles now separated them, her dad still loved her just as much as he always had, if not more. He was still a source of joy.

And Dick, well, he sat back in his chair and shed a few tears of his own, moved by remembrances of his little girl and the knowledge that she still wanted to be his pot of gold.

"To this day, whenever I hear a song my daddy used to sing, tears come to my eyes."

❦ SIMPLE TRADITIONS ❧

GRETA'S FATHER WAS a railroad engineer. As such, he traveled great distances and could be away from home for long stretches at a time. For this reason, and due to the demands of her new job, Greta didn't get to see her dad as much as she wanted now that she had completed college and begun her career.

In between their visits, she often thought back to mornings of her childhood when they would stroll along the sidewalk, holding hands, making their way to a coffee shop to meet some of his railroad buddies. Being together while her dad had a cup of coffee was a beloved tradition for them. At home they were always the first to get up and quietly make his coffee while they talked softly, waiting for the rest of the family to roll out of bed.

Trips to the coffee shop were a special treat for Greta. Marcus, her dad, would buy her anything she wanted from the pastry case. He'd chuckle as she called the railroaders by their nicknames, as if they were her old friends instead of his. In this setting, Greta became intrigued with trains. Trains and coffee were the things that tied her to her dad.

The day she moved into her new third-floor office, Greta noticed an elevated railroad track running alongside the building. Curious, she called her dad and asked if he ever traveled that track. "Only a few times a year," he said. She made him promise, if he were ever to pass by, that he would call and let her know so she could go to the window and wave to him.

She told her new co-workers about her father's promise, and thereafter each day when a train went by, someone would tease her, calling out, "Is that your daddy?" Each time she had to give the same, disappointed answer: "No." Soon, she began to dislike the sound of trains.

Late one afternoon while she was sitting at her desk, her cell phone started to vibrate in her pocket. As she pulled it out and answered, she heard the noise of a train engine in the background.

"Guess where I am?" her dad hollered into the phone.

Greta heard the low roar of the train, this time from outside her office, and she felt the floor vibrate under her feet. Her dad's train was rolling into town! Excited, she called out to her co-workers that her dad's train was finally coming around the bend. Everyone went to the bank of windows overlooking the tracks and watched.

As the train got closer, a door in the engineer's cabin opened, and out onto the little platform walked her dad, holding a mug of coffee. He smiled, raising his mug to toast his beloved daughter as he spotted her across the way. He waved as the train passed by and continued to wave until he could no longer see her face pressed against the office window.

Greta returned to her desk with a renewed smile, not only because her co-workers would finally stop teasing her, but because her dad had kept his promise, just as he always had. She sat facing the window and listened intently to the sound outside, steel wheels on a railroad track, until the last squeal could be heard.

"The first time I saw a grey hair on his head, my heart skipped a beat. My dad was getting older, and someday I would lose him."

⁓ THE MEAGAN BOX ⁓

ON THE COVER of my first book, there's a picture of, among other things, a letter I wrote to Meagan when she was in kindergarten. On my way to the airport for a weeklong business trip, I dropped the letter off at her school, wanting to give her something to comfort her during my absence. It read, "I love you more than peanut butter, sunshine, and ice cream." I have kept that letter in a cardboard box in my closet—a memory box I affectionately call the Meagan Box.

Also in the Meagan Box are samples of her best artwork I've collected over the years, her first pair of shoes, her first ballet slippers, and my childhood hairbrush my mother saved and then gave me to use with Meagan. This cardboard box is full of the things that trigger some of my favorite memories.

Another dad told me of a time when he was spring cleaning and found a little pink baseball cap in his closet. The cap belonged to his daughter, and he remembered her wearing it as she ran around the house, her hair flopping wildly from underneath the cap. Holding that cap, he wanted to turn back the clock, even if for only a few minutes, to the days when he could pick her up and hold her in the air, refusing to put her down until she promised to give him three sweet kisses and a hug.

The memories daughters and dads have of their relationships not only remind them of what the relationships once were, but also give them hope for what they have yet to become. Now I have a stepdaughter, Linley, in my life, and I hope that my best days with both my girls are not behind me. Instead, I believe our past predicts what great things we will do and enjoy together over the rest of our lives.

This year when my birthday rolled around, I asked the girls not to purchase anything for me; what I wanted was a letter from each of them. They argued with me and insisted that gifts, especially new clothing, were a better idea, pointing to my shirt and suggesting I clearly didn't know how to shop for myself.

I explained to my fashion consultants that clothing doesn't last; things wear out or get lost. But a letter will last my lifetime; I can read it when I'm old, nearing death and taking account of what my life amounted to. I would keep them in the Meagan Box and the new box I've started for letters and cards from Linley.

I eventually convinced them of the sincerity of my request, and I did receive two wonderful letters for my birthday. As I put them in their respective memory boxes, I read Meagan's letter once more. She ended it with, "You've given the world to me, and I hope I can give it back to you."

"You just did, honey," I whispered, folding it carefully and slipping it between the pages of her baby book.

A dad wants his daughters' reassurance

just as much as they want his.

⌁ TO THE RESCUE ⌁

WHILE GETTING OFF the bus one morning on the way to elementary school, Alice tried to jump across a snow-and-ice-covered curb. Unlike her fellow students who had jumped before her and cleared the icy patch, eight-year-old Alice didn't leap quite far enough, and down she went. One of her hands bent backward as she landed, and the force snapped her wrist.

Although she was in considerable pain, she didn't shed a tear as she was escorted to the school nurse's office. She wanted to be a brave girl, as brave as her father always was.

The nurse called Alice's parents to tell them of her accident and learned that the stoic child would have to wait until her mother could find someone to drive them there to pick her up. Both parents were blind and obviously could not drive themselves to the school.

Her father hadn't yet left the house for work when the nurse's call came in, and wanting to be with his injured daughter as soon as possible, he decided not to wait for a ride. He grabbed his cane and left the house, in his haste leaving his gloves and scarf behind. He walked just over a mile through the Philadelphia winter, all the way to the school.

When her father walked into the nurse's office, Alice burst into tears, not because the pain of her broken wrist had finally gotten to her, but because she was so touched that her dad had endured the walk to come to her side dressed only in his business suit. In spite of his vision impairment and in the face of rather unfavorable conditions, he had once more come to her rescue.

He took a seat beside her, draped his arm around her shoulders, and kissed her on top of her head. "You're going to be okay," he said, "Daddy's here." He carefully raised his fingers to her cheeks and brushed away the tears he knew were there.

Alice knew that day that nothing could stop her dad; he would come to her rescue whenever she needed him to. And over the following years he did.

~ A SCENT OF DAD ~

AMY'S PARENTS DIVORCED long before joint custody became the norm. Consequently, she lived with her mother. Missing her dad as much as she did between their brief visits, she often cried herself to sleep. With her face in her pillow to muffle her sobs, she hoped for a genie lamp or time-travel machine, anything that would instantly bring her daddy near to her even though he was miles away.

Never finding such a thing under her pillow, Amy decided to take a more practical approach.

At that time, her dad, Stanley, wore English Leather cologne, and Amy knew it came packaged in a wooden box. One day she asked him for one of the wooden boxes, and he gave it to her. She continued to ask for more boxes as the weeks and months went by, and each time her dad complied.

Once, as he handed her yet another one, Stanley asked what she kept in all those boxes. That was when he learned his daughter didn't put anything in the boxes; instead she kept the freshest-smelling one under her pillow or inside the top drawer of her bedside table. Any time she missed him, she grabbed it, opened it, and breathed in the scent of her dad. It wasn't him in the flesh, but it would get her through until the next time she would see him.

Stanley continued to wear English Leather for years even though he knew it had long gone out of style. Whenever Amy asked for another wooden box, there was always one ready to offer.

Dads and daughters are always
on each other's minds.

❧ A FATHER'S PLACE ❧

JOHNNY, MY FATHER-IN-LAW, is very attached to his only daughter, often telling me, "Jill will always be my little girl." Before I met Jill, he spent a considerable amount of time helping her with whatever she needed, including cutting the grass and making repairs at her home, keeping up with the maintenance of her car, and picking up Linley, his granddaughter, after school.

Eager to make a good impression on my girlfriend and her parents, I began to take over the lawn care and home-repair tasks shortly after our first date. Johnny was supposed to be enjoying his retirement years, I reasoned, not laboring outside in the heat pushing a lawn mower or climbing a ladder.

In spite of my reassurances that I didn't need his help, Johnny made surprise appearances on the days I planned to work at Jill's house. He insisted on helping me prune the shrubs and advised me on how to secure a loose board in the dining-room floor. He continued to show up and work alongside me throughout my courtship of Jill, sometimes even arriving before I did to begin the work himself, right up to the day we made the buyer's final requested improvements to the house. Jill had sold it so we could move into the new home we had purchased together.

Once Jill and I married, I became the master of my domicile. Now I did all the yard work and home repairs, got the oil changed in my wife's car, and began shuttling Linley back and forth to and from school.

Johnny kept asking me if I needed his help, and I kept politely answering no. I didn't want to burden him with what I thought I should be doing for my new blended family.

One day I reluctantly asked Johnny to come by and water our recently landscaped front yard while we were out of town on vacation. He, of course, eagerly agreed. After I hung up the phone, Jill pulled me aside. "Thank you," she said.

I looked at her, clueless about why she was thanking me.

"He wants to help; he likes to do things for *me*."

That's when I finally understood. Johnny wasn't inserting himself into my world; he was maintaining his place in Jill's. He only wanted to continue to be a daddy to his little girl.

Today Johnny and I work together to keep our yard and house in top shape and to take good care of Jill and Linley. And ever the dad, he now does things for Meagan and me too. We are *all* just as delighted to receive his help as he is to give it.

All dads want to hold on to their places
in their little girls' lives.

❧

༺ THE SOFTIE ༻

WANDA, SIX YEARS OLD, sat in her room, astonished about what had just happened—her mom had sent her to bed without dinner. As she tried to figure out what she could have done that was so wrong and worthy of such cruel punishment, her bedroom door quietly opened. She looked up and saw her dad standing there, his finger to his lips and holding a small cardboard box.

He carefully crept across the room, taking care not to make the floor creak, sat down on the bed next to his daughter, and opened the box. Inside was the largest vanilla cupcake she had ever seen, one that was coated thick with tempting white frosting and colorful candy sprinkles. She looked into her dad's face for a clue as to why he would be torturing her like this. Surely he knew she was hungry!

He gave a mischievous smile, nodded toward the cupcake, but didn't speak a word. She understood then that he was sneaking it in to give her a little snack—dessert no less.

As Wanda ate every crumb of that cupcake, making sure to lick all the icing from her fingers, her dad patted her leg and reassured her she was not alone in her misbehavior. He said he understood that no one could possibly follow all the rules all the time. After all, no one is perfect. He certainly wasn't, and he wouldn't expect more from her than from himself.

That evening, even though he may not have realized it at the time, Curtis taught his daughter not only what was reasonable to expect from others but also just how much she should expect from herself—not perfection, but her very best.

Dads don't expect
their daughters to be perfect.

⌣ SHARED SADNESS ⌣

IT HAD BEEN a hard few years for Virginia. Painful and emotionally draining health problems eventually led to the onset of a debilitating depression. Worries about her family, her health, and her seemingly bleak future kept her in a dark mood; nothing could lift her spirits. Some days she did little more than sit, worry, and cry.

One afternoon her dad came to her home for a visit and found her in bed, a wad of tear-soaked tissues on her nightstand and nothing but misery on her face. Seeing his daughter in such a state was more than the seventy-eight-year-old father could bear. Not knowing what he should do to help her but desperately wanting to do something to bring back the smiling face of his precious little girl, he did the only thing he could think of—he took off his shoes, climbed into bed beside her, and wrapped his arms around her. They lay there and cried together.

⌇GIRLS GROW UP⌇

WHEN FOUR-YEAR-OLD Lily first became aware that her dad, Warren, left home each morning to go to work and would then be out of sight for hours, she cried if she had not waved good-bye to him. To offer comfort and minimize Lily's tears, Mom began waking her each morning in time to stand in her bedroom window and wave good-bye as Dad backed his car out of the garage.

Lily waved to her dad every workday for two years; that's how long it took for her to believe he really would be coming home at the end of each day. When he finally did walk through the door, she dropped everything to run to him and jump into his open arms.

Although Warren was relieved when he learned his little girl had outgrown her fear of his disappearance, he couldn't help but be a little saddened the first morning he looked up and saw an empty window at Lily's bedroom. It was her first step toward that moment he knew was coming but hoped was still many years away—when little girls become teens and have little time and affection for their dads.

Steering his car onto the road, Warren remembered the previous morning when Lily had waved good-bye to him. Had he known it would be the last time she would send him off in that way, he would have paused and watched her a little longer, looking at the twinkle in her eyes, knowing he was the reason she was up so early.

As he reassured himself that he still held a special place in his daughter's heart, he hoped she had not also outgrown the afternoon greeting she offered him upon his return home. *That* he was not yet ready to lose. It was his favorite part of the day.

"Boys show dads love in their own unique, if oblique, way. Daughters, on the other hand, give hugs and kisses and say, "I love you, Daddy" almost without reservation. To be a daughter's dad is to experience a joy beyond comparison."

⌁ DAD'S FAVORITE WORDS ⌁

MEAGAN AND I spent a day on the University of Georgia campus, where she hopes to attend next year. We toured the classrooms and stadium, met with a few faculty members, and peeked into a freshman-women's dorm, where I had to explain that the stack of menus on the foyer table were not for room service but were from the local restaurants that offered dorm delivery. After our tour, we went to lunch at a café near campus, and I entertained her with stories about how much fun my two cousins and I'd had years ago while attending the same university.

Before long I noticed that my staunchly self-reliant, independent teenager sitting quietly across the table from me was fiddling with her salad. "Is something wrong?" I asked.

"Will you come visit me?" she asked.

"Of course I will," I answered. "At least once a week."

She started to choke on her arugula. "Ah, that's a bit much," she managed to get out.

It didn't matter. My little girl had just told me she would miss me when she left home. We would reach an agreement later about how often I would be "permitted" to come to visit, but for the moment I got something I had been hoping for—reassurance she did not think leaving home would also mean leaving me behind.

Over the previous couple of years, as Meagan had become more independent, she'd also become less willing to turn to me for what she needed and even less willing to accept my affection. I tried to convince her I should be permitted to hug and kiss her at will; I was, after all, her father. She didn't budge, and it took me too long to realize my persistence only solidified her conviction. The more I tried to maintain our affection, the less of it I received.

I'm not sure how I finally got the point, but eventually I did, and my gestures of affection were replaced with text messages and occasional brief hugs. I preferred more, but I was learning to be happy with what I could get. Any affection was better than none.

By the time of this lunch, I had begun to worry about what place I would have in her life after she left home. I thought she was eager to get away from me, a dad who all too often had been accused of hovering far too much.

Just days before, I had received an e-mail from a twenty-three-year-old woman who admitted that, although she only lived fifteen minutes from her parents' home, law school consumed nearly all her time, and she rarely saw her family. What little free time she did have she spent with her fiancé. She wanted advice on how to help her dad understand that things were changing between them; she loved him still but just couldn't see him as often as he wished.

It seems her dad was having a difficult time dealing with the realization that within a year his daughter would graduate from law school, begin her career, get married, and live as an adult. I recognized his quandary—he thought he was losing his little girl.

Strangers we were, that father and I, yet we had something in common—we did not want to go through the pain that seems to follow the distance all daughters eventually place between themselves and their fathers.

Fortunately, the inevitable quest for independence does not signal the end of the daughter-dad relationship. My friend, Edward, reassured me of this as he shared his memories of his own relationship with Amber, his determined and independent daughter.

He, like any good dad, tried to discourage his teenage daughter's willful behavior, rewarding good conduct and issuing consequences for the bad, including grounding her and denying her favorite privileges. She simply dealt with him in her usual determined way, which more often than not meant she simply ignored him and did what she wanted anyway.

Amber entered her college years with great enthusiasm. With mixed emotions, Edward drove his daughter off to college, convinced it was the beginning of the end of their tenuous relationship.

As he expected, Amber's phone calls home were few and far between. Some days he even wondered if his only role in her life was to pay tuition. Four years went by quickly, and then one day he found himself on campus to watch his daughter graduate. It was then he noticed that something about Amber seemed to have changed. She appeared happy to see him and even touched him as they spoke. Afterward, she began calling home, sometimes with specific objectives in mind, other times just to talk about anything that was on her dad's mind.

One day she asked for his advice as she launched her first professional job search. When she landed that dream job, she called her dad before anyone else to thank him for his advice and encouragement. Soon, she began to say other things Edward thought he would never hear but had held out hope for.

After she moved into her own apartment, Amber started talking with her dad more regularly than she did back when she lived under his roof. She started visiting home every Sunday night for dinner, and in time she sent her dad an e-mail thanking him for being her "best friend."

His story gave me hope that one day Meagan, too, would send me such an e-mail. My thoughts returned to the law student who had written me a few days earlier. She had said, "I will always need him, even though he is no longer the only man in my life. Actually, I need him now more than ever."

"Then go tell him," I wrote back. "I'm sure there's nothing else he'd rather hear you say."

"She's leaving home soon. When that happens, I don't know what I'll do with myself."

❦ DADDY-DAUGHTER DATES ❧

CRAIG DECIDED TO start a date-night tradition in order to spend one-on-one time with each of his daughters. He let them choose where they wanted to go from a variety of options he had determined he could endure. They usually chose one of those pizza-and-arcade places with mechanized animals that annoy the adults but delight the children.

In the daughters' early years, there wasn't a lot of meaningful conversation between them and Dad, but it didn't matter to Craig. For him the dates were more about spending time together doing something the girls wanted to do.

As the years went by and their recreational preferences changed, the girls began to choose movies, grown-up restaurants, horseback riding, bowling, and the like for their date nights. Topics of conversation changed too. They began to share with their dad the problems they were dealing with at school or among their friends. Those were the times when he felt most connected to his daughters, when he could help them solve their most pressing problems.

As things go, each daughter in her own time eventually reached an age when daddy-daughter dates fell out of favor. Craig, saddened, had only memories of dates past to comfort him when he missed spending time with his daughters.

A time came when Craig and his wife drove to the university their oldest daughter attended; they were to accompany her to a parents' weekend event hosted by her sorority. After enjoying dinner with several of her friends and their families, Craig was surprised by his daughter's request that he go out on a date with her.

It had been a long time since they'd had a date. Craig's wife knew how much the request meant to him, so she encouraged him to go. Soon, he found himself in a pub where his daughter enjoyed hanging out with her college friends. They laughed, teased each other, and played pool for hours, beating everyone who dared challenge the duo.

Finally, many pool games later and long after when he would have normally gone to bed, Craig drove his daughter back to her dorm. Before she went inside, they sat in the car to talk just a bit longer. That was when she told her dad how proud she was of him and that she had asked for the date because she wanted her friends to know what a great dad she had.

As he sat in the car and watched his daughter walk to her dorm, he realized how tired he was but at the same time was certain he could have played a few more games of pool had she asked him to.

Craig slept peacefully that night, his heart lifted by the best compliment he had received in a long time and the hope that he wouldn't have to wait long for his next invitation to a daddy-daughter date.

⌇SURPRISING SUPPORTER⌇

KEITH, A DAD in California, picked up his thirteen-year-old daughter, Heidi, from school one afternoon. During their conversation on the drive home, he learned she was going to run for class president. Her competition was only the most popular boy in the class, she said. She admitted to being nervous but thought she had a chance of winning because the most popular girls in her class had assured her she had their votes. It seems the young man had fallen out of their favor since he began dating a young lady from another school.

Like any father, Keith bristled when hearing his daughter talk about "the popular girls." He tried to get her to explain who they were and why they were "popular," and she finally confided that they were popular because they were very pretty. All the boys had crushes on them.

Keith wanted to say so many things to his daughter then about what true beauty really means, but having previously had a number of perfectly rational but unfruitful conversations with her on other subjects that concerned her, he thought he'd have no better luck on this topic.

So instead, as any father well practiced in the avoidance of a teen girl's ire would do, he asked if she wanted to get her hair cut and styled in preparation for the upcoming elections. Heidi didn't hesitate a moment and said yes.

They went to four different salons that Friday afternoon before they found someone who could squeeze her in. As his daughter took her place in the salon chair, Keith gave her free reign to do whatever she wanted with her hair.

Heidi promptly told the stylist how she wanted her hair done. Once a hair-makeover plan was finalized, Dad was informed it would take about two hours to complete.

Keith tried to pass the time by walking around window-shopping, but he eventually ended up back at the salon. He sat in a chair under a dome dryer, which probably looked funny because he is nearly bald with only short stubble adorning his head.

If his daughter is anything like mine, I'm sure she rolled her eyes and silently wished for invisibility upon spying her dad under that dryer.

It didn't matter to Keith that his daughter might have been embarrassed by him, because, two and a half hours later, her hair makeover was finished. He looked at her and saw an absolutely beautiful young girl, not because she had a new hair style, but because she had a confident, radiant smile on her face.

Keith is not one who thinks beauty can be bought, manufactured, or fixed; rather, he believes that beauty comes from within the heart and soul of the woman. Yet he learned something valuable that day in his pursuit of understanding his daughter—what she thought about her own beauty at her impressionable age was just as important as what he thought about it.

On that day Keith discovered a new kind of beauty—the look of a young girl confident in her appearance. On that day, he watched his once little darling in pigtails begin her journey toward becoming a woman.

_____

Even when they don't entirely understand it,
dads help their daughters become
who they want to be.

_____

↝ WHAT'S REALLY IMPORTANT ↜

ASHLEY IS NOT quite six years old and attends kindergarten. Her mom and dad, both full-time professionals, have very busy work schedules and toil long hours to build a comfortable future for their family. Yet, in spite of their ambition, they make spending time with Ashley a priority, beginning with their first activity of the day. Each morning they pray together as a family, thanking God for their blessings, then they walk to the street corner to stand with Ashley until she has boarded the school bus.

To make sure they do not let their careers get in the way of doing fun things with Ashley, the parents also take turns leaving their jobs early. Each has assigned days to greet Ashley at the bus stop and then spend time helping her do homework, playing, or doing whatever else pleases their little girl.

Ashley's father, Nathan, an executive with a worldwide corporate endeavor, most often spends his summer afternoons with his daughter at the community pool, but one afternoon Ashley decided she wanted to do something different for a change. Skipping their usual trip to the pool, they grabbed a bucket of art supplies and began to redecorate their driveway instead.

After half an hour of tempera painting and drawing with chalk on the concrete, Ashley looked up at her dad and smiled. "Playing with you like this is much better than being at the pool with everyone else," she said.

There were times when Nathan worried that leaving work early would compromise his career; he might not be there when needed to fix a pressing problem or close a big sale. But that afternoon, playing with Ashley in the driveway, he was convinced that no problem or deal could be more important than succeeding as a father. Knowing his priorities were in order, he vowed they would stay that way.

∽: THE RELUCTANT LET-GO :∽

THERE WAS A time when Meagan needed me for everything. I taught her how to tie her shoes, buckle her seat belt, and use the microwave oven. Soon, she wanted me to show her how to make her own scrambled eggs and shuffle a deck of cards and, eventually, drive a car.

As she mastered these tasks and continued to grow up, becoming more independent and less willing to turn to me for what she wanted or needed, I knew the worst was yet to come. I braced myself for when she would no longer kiss me on the lips or allow me to accompany her to a doctor visit.

I had been her facilitator and protector, doing all the things she couldn't do for herself and training her for independence by gradually giving her more freedom but not before issuing appropriate warnings. That, too, was a time-limited role, and soon I was admonished for not trusting her. One day she asked— rather, demanded of me—"Don't you want to see if I've learned anything from you?" I really had no choice but to shut my mouth, say a little prayer, and take a somewhat reluctant step backward.

Just a few days later I took her to the airport for her first solo flight.

Once at the airport, I got her bag out of the car and sent her off to check herself in, a task she was determined to do on her own. We hugged and said good-bye, and she headed into the airport terminal.

The temptation to follow her was great, but I kept my feet firmly planted and watched only until she looked over her shoulder to wave one last time. I got in my car and drove off, confident she was checking herself in and finding her way toward the security gates. I imagined her boarding the shuttle that would carry her to the departure gate, finding her seat, and then loading her bag into the overhead compartment.

Twenty minutes away from the airport, my phone rang; Meagan called to assure me all went well and she was safely onboard. I smiled, proud and admittedly a little relieved. She said, "I love you," twice before hanging up, and I smiled again, only then more happily.

Letting go of my little girl is one of the most difficult, and yet at the same time the most rewarding, things I've ever done.

·∻ THE FIRST MAN IN HER LIFE ∻·

ON A HOT and sticky Tennessee Sunday morning, seventeen-year-old Kristen was sitting beside her dad, Phil, at a church camp. Having just eaten breakfast, he was about to call his wife back home to see how she was doing.

A youth pastor for twenty-two years, Phil had organized the weeklong church camp. With one hundred teenagers under his charge already, another six hundred teens from other churches were on their way to join in the activities. Kristen, his only daughter, had accompanied him on the trip.

Phil had a close-knit family of five, but at the moment Kristen was the child who caused him the most concern. She had been dating a young man for some time, and he was not one Phil heartily approved of. Although he seemed to be a nice and well-behaved teen, he possessed certain personality traits that Phil believed undermined the values he had worked hard to instill in each of his children.

Phil and his wife spent many nights in prayer, asking that the perfect companion for Kristen be sent to her.

When he made that phone call home, Phil discovered a terrible storm had ravaged their community. His wife burst into tears as she told him of the trees that lay in their yard and the damage done to their roof. The power was out with no promise of its being restored for days.

As resourceful as his wife was, she didn't know where he kept the flashlights. He wanted to go to her, but he had hundreds of young people looking to him for his leadership during that week. After some thought and prayer, he decided to leave camp and go to his wife.

Quickly making new arrangements with the adult volunteers who were there to help him run the camp, he jumped into his car to head home. He drove over six hours to get home, while Kristen stayed behind to help with the camp.

It was well after dark when Phil arrived home. He spent much of that night and the next morning clearing the yard of fallen limbs and making emergency repairs to the house. As the afternoon approached, he kissed his wife good-bye and, even though he was nearly exhausted, drove back to the camp, arriving in time for evening devotions. He reassured those from his community who gathered around that their families and homes were safe.

As the group prepared to end the evening service, they turned to the Prayer Box. Each teen had a secret prayer partner for whom he or she left notes that were to be handed out each night. As Phil passed out the notes, he came across a folded piece of paper with his name on it. He recognized the handwriting as he opened the note; it was from Kristen.

Dear Dad,

Thank you for loving our family. I know it was hard for you to leave camp yesterday. When you went home, I knew that we mean more to you than anything else. You left the camp you had worked for months to organize to go home and attend to your family.

I want to marry a man who will love me and our children just like you love us. Thank you for helping me to realize that.

I love you,
Kristen

Shortly after returning home from camp, Kristen broke up with her boyfriend.

Not surprisingly, the next young man to come into Kristen's life was the one Phil and his wife had prayed for all those nights. When Alex asked Phil for permission to marry Kristen, Phil, of course, agreed. Alex has turned out to be just the man whom Kristen, and her parents, were looking for.

A father shows his daughter how she should expect to be treated by other men.

↜ IN DADDY'S EYES ↝

WHEN CAITLYN WAS just four years old, her mother looked down and saw that one of her blue eyes had started turning toward her nose. Together they marched into a Washington optometrist's office, and a couple of hours later, Caitlyn had her first pair of glasses.

Unfortunately, those glasses were neither sleek nor stylish. Even worse than being about as thick as the bottom of a soda bottle, they were bifocals too. During the drive home her mom tried to encourage Caitlyn to think positively about wearing glasses, but Caitlyn dreaded what she was certain her friends would say when they saw her wearing those massive, ugly bifocals.

But more than she feared what her friends might say, Caitlyn worried about how her dad would react to the change of her appearance.

That evening when her dad arrived home from work, Caitlyn shied away and tried to hide her face. Having gotten an advance notice from mom about his daughter's worry, he sat down at the kitchen table and called her to his side. She nervously stood before him as he took a long look at her face and studied her glasses. Then, with the utmost conviction and authority, he said, "You look beautiful. Go to the mirror and see for yourself; you're a movie star."

Caitlyn walked sheepishly into the bathroom and gazed into the mirror, repeating to herself her father's words, "You look beautiful." Turning her head from side to side, looking at her face and glasses from all possible angles, she finally smiled.

"I do look like a movie star," she told herself.

Any feelings of self-doubt and insecurity were swept away as she repeated her father's words over and over again. When she turned away from the mirror, she was ready to deal with anything that anybody might have to say about her glasses. Her dad thought she was beautiful in spite of those bifocals, and his opinion on that subject was the only one that mattered to her.

As she looks back at photographs from those days, Caitlyn sees that she looked nothing like a movie star. But in that simple conversation that occurred twenty-eight years ago, her dad did more than reassure her about her appearance. He let her know that in his eyes she would always be beautiful. He would always see the best in her.

⌣ THEY MEAN WELL ⌣

AT THE AGE of twenty-four, Haley was the youngest of eleven children, four of whom were adopted. Fifteen years separated Haley from her oldest sibling, and as many as eight children lived in their home at any one time. While one might expect the youngest child to get lost in such a crowded house, Haley was a standout. In fact, as she tells it, she is her father's favorite child.

Thomas, her father, was the sole provider for the family; he worked a lot, often six days a week. His children, and in particular a young Haley, sometimes felt as though they did not see him very much. When he was able to spend time at home, reading a book in an attempt to relax or just sitting before the television in his favorite chair was foremost on his mind.

However, in spite of his fatigue, he knew he needed to pay attention to his youngest daughter. She made it clear to all that she wanted more of his time. Giving her his undivided attention was a challenge; there was always a rowdy audience in the house. To spend time alone with Haley, he would seek her out, tap her on the shoulder, and ask, "Do you want to go with me?" If she bothered to ask where he was going, his response was direct, "It's a yes or no question; do you want to go with me?"

Haley nearly always answered, "Yes."

Sometimes their outings meant going to his office where Haley played in the big open spaces of the uniform-cleaning plant while Dad attended to his paperwork. Other times he took her to visit his brothers and sisters or the neighborhood where he grew up. Either location was a perfect setting for telling stories about his youth. Haley loved to hear about her father's life as a young boy.

Thomas also planned fun things for the pair to do together. Often they went fishing or to a farm where they could pick their own watermelon and cantaloupe. Sometimes they stopped at farms or pet shops to look at animals, in particular kittens. One day, after who knows how much pestering, he finally relented and allowed Haley to get a cat, even though he himself had no use for one.

Haley didn't care much about what they would be doing on their daughter-dad outings. As busy as her father was, he had made time to spend exclusively with her, and his undivided attention was what she wanted most. The time they spent together in those days would be remembered later when a teenaged Haley sat beside her father's hospital bed as he struggled to recover from an aneurism.

In the early years of her adolescence, Haley had thought her dad was far too strict. In her mind, he didn't understand her at all and didn't seem to try. Feeling like they could no longer talk with each other, even at times thinking he didn't love her anymore, she had begun doing what she could to avoid her dad.

But there in the hospital Haley thought of her cat and days past spent fishing or riding into the country to pick melons when she was Thomas's little tagalong. There was no time to waste being distant from her father now, a man with a heart big enough to raise eleven children, a man who called each child his favorite and could make them all feel as though they were.

After her father recovered and returned home, Haley set about to improve her relationship with him. She wanted to feel again the affectionate attachment that had once characterized their relationship.

At that time, Haley was one of only two children still living at home. Her brother had graduated from high school and was rarely around, so Haley was often alone with her parents. Thomas, slowed by his medical condition, began to spend more time at home. Monday nights became family night, an evening set aside for the three to spend time with one another.

Haley began to joke around with her dad, including teasing him about how even though he "hated" the cat, he always brought home table scraps for Butch whenever they dined out. During that teasing, they discovered they shared a wicked sense of humor and an appreciation for sarcastic wit.

After Thomas fully recovered, he and Haley began to go on outings again. Today he continues to call her his favorite child, and he still brings leftovers home for the cat.

And for Haley—those feelings of attachment to her dad have returned and are now stronger than ever. They still tease each other, but they also say, "I love you," more often than ever before.

"Once I wanted to find a husband who wouldn't be anything like my dad. Now all I hope for is to find a husband who will be just like my dad."

✌: THE FOUNDATION :✌

ALTHOUGH MEAGAN WAS driving pretty well by the time she got her learner's permit, she still had a few skills to master, like judging how close the car was to the curb. One afternoon, when she was still in training, I had to tell her several times to steer toward the center of the lane. She ignored my direction and insisted I was worried about nothing. Just then she slammed into a curb while rounding a curve in the road.

As the car began what at the time seemed like its second revolution of a triple axel, I saw hot coffee sloshing over the rim of the cup I was trying desperately not to tip over. I heard myself screaming like a girl as I realized my delicate region was drowning in steaming java, and then I heard Meagan's laughter as she managed to regain control of the car.

"Dad, you look like you wet your pants," she said. "And don't leave your coffee cup in my car," she warned. This coming from the girl who for years had left gum wrappers, used tissue, eye-liner-pencil shavings, nail clippings, and spilled Skittles all over my car.

I remembered giving Meagan driving lessons when she was only ten years old. Using remote, open fields for roadways, I tried to give her as much driving experience as possible before she would set out behind the wheel by herself. One afternoon while visiting my parents, who live in a small, sleepy country town, I decided it was time to let her steer onto the open road.

Earlier in the afternoon, I had been sitting on the front porch with my mom, sharing with her my frustrations about how Meagan seemed to enjoy my company less than she once did. She was becoming a young woman, one who was certain her dad had no idea what she was going through, one who was turning to confidants other than me to spend time and share her thoughts with.

"You need to find a new way to relate with her," my mom had said. "She isn't a little girl anymore." I was thinking of this advice when I directed my then-thirteen-year-old to turn off the dirt road and onto the two-lane blacktop.

She ignored one stop sign and ran onto the shoulder of the road twice, but no one was injured or killed, although she did narrowly miss running over a chicken innocently trying to cross the road.

We spent the next three years practicing driving on the roadways instead of in open fields. It was time well spent, I think. Not only was she a safer driver by the time she got her own car (save for the curb incident), but it was time we spent working together toward a common goal. Even if she was upset with me, I could always gain her company with one simple question: "Do you want to go driving?"

Jill and I sat on our front porch one evening and watched the road in front of our house, waiting for Meagan. She finally turned the corner and slowly approached our driveway; windows were down, sunroof open, and music blaring.

She had just driven away from her mom's house, ending up at mine only ten miles later, completing her first solo drive. She sat on the porch and talked with Jill and me for a while but didn't stay long; her boyfriend's home was her next stop. She hugged us both as she got up to leave and then carefully backed out of our driveway, using the blinker and looking both ways before entering the street.

I wasn't offended when she left after such a short visit; I was happy she had come to see me first.

The experiences of life are the foundation on which the father-daughter relationship is built.

ᴖ REASSURED ᴖ

AFTER JUST FINISHING an interview for a new position within her company, Doreen sat back down at her desk. The position would be an important promotion for her, one she thought she was ready for, one she really wanted. She opened her e-mail with a sigh, uneasy with her performance in the interview.

Scanning her in-box, her eyes came to rest on one e-mail in particular; it was from her dad. Although he held an executive position with a large broadcasting company, he was more of a cowboy and handyman than a technology wizard. To receive an e-mail from him was a big surprise and a meaningful event in itself. He could install a toilet, repair a garage-door opener, or build a new deck on the house, but he was all thumbs at a computer keyboard.

"I have been thinking about you," his message began.

He went on at length to tell her of his own experiences seeking promotions throughout his career, of his successes and failures, and of what he had learned about himself and others along the way. He spoke of pride, disappointment, courage, and character and about appreciating the knowledge and experiences life gives us.

He reassured his daughter he was proud of her simply because she was being considered for the new position. It didn't matter to him whether she received the promotion or not. He already knew, he wrote, what his daughter was made of—she possessed all the qualities and traits he believed truly mattered in life.

He signed his e-mail simply: "I love you, Daddy."

Doreen leaned back in her chair and smiled, now not caring too much about the outcome of the interview. She had been promoted, as far as she was concerned, by her dad, a professional she had always revered. If he wasn't disappointed in her, she wouldn't be either.

"His quiet strength instilled in me a sense
of security that has served as both
my anchor and rudder throughout my life."

⋆ CHANGES ⋆

A FATHER TOLD of his young daughter's coming home from school, bounding with excitement. It seems a bottom front tooth that had been loose for days had finally flopped forward and was now barely hanging on.

After much prompting to halt her hopping and squirming, he tried to pull that loose tooth the rest of the way out, but his fingers were too big to grasp just the one tooth. Mom reached in and quickly plucked it out, relieving their daughter from what she had by then convinced herself was going to be the most excruciating experience of her life.

Mom got teary-eyed, and Dad admitted he felt a twitch in his eyes, but it didn't last more than a moment. No melancholy could have withstood the joy of watching his daughter dancing and singing about the brand-new gap in her smile. She ran from mirror to mirror to study the dark red hole in her gum and test how much of her tongue she could push between her teeth.

He helped his daughter rinse her mouth out with warm salt water just as his dad had him do when he lost his first tooth. He took a few minutes of video to commemorate the occasion and then tucked her into bed. A few hours later, the tooth fairy made a visit, slipped a five-dollar bill under the frilly pillow, and kissed her gently on the forehead.

Later that evening, Dad reassured his wife that nothing had fundamentally changed in their world; it was just a tooth. Yet all the while he wrestled with his own mix of joy and fear after witnessing this sign that to him meant his little girl was growing up.

I well remember encountering such signs.

Once puberty struck, change in my relationship with Meagan was inevitable. I understood the need for change, although that didn't make it any easier to accept. I knew that emotional distance followed soon after physical distance. We were on the cusp of a separation I dreaded.

One day while doing laundry, as I reached into the washing machine to pull out the load of clothes she had started but left unfinished, I saw what I thought was the leg of a stuffed animal. It was a leopard, I decided, peeking out from the knot of clothes that was twisted around the washer's agitator. As I grabbed it to pull it out, it suddenly occurred to me that Meagan didn't have a stuffed leopard.

That was when I realized I was holding a thong, a piece of fabric not even big enough to blow my nose in. I nearly passed out. Meagan walked in, saw what I held in my hand, and reached out to grab it. "Don't say a word," she warned and shooed me away from the laundry room.

Some days I long for the return of the tooth fairy.

FULFILLING
ᴗHOPES AND DREAMSᴗ

MICHAEL, SOMEWHAT JADED by his years in the military followed by a career investigating crime scenes, had grown weary of the traditional Christmas celebrations. The season had gotten overcommercialized and lost its heart, he thought. Gift-giving delighted his children but didn't provide him with what he wanted most, an opportunity to spend quality time with his family, focusing only on one another and creating memories that would last a lifetime.

One evening during dinner, after listening to his daughters chatter on about what they wanted Santa to bring them that year, he announced his plan for the family to begin traveling during the winter holiday. Each year, he explained, they would enjoy spending time together exploring a new destination and getting to know one another better.

Although Elizabeth and Caroline didn't like the idea of traveling during Christmas at first, they soon grew to eagerly antici-pate where their dad would take them next as each winter break drew near. St. Louis, Phoenix, Beverly Hills perhaps?

One December, Michael took his family to Seattle to enjoy a truly white Christmas. Among the events he had planned for his family was a hike into the nearby foothills to enjoy gazing at the glaciated peaks of Mount Rainier in the distance. It would be the first time his daughters, who had been raised on the beaches of Florida, would see snowcapped mountains.

The afternoon before the day of the hike, the family members found themselves in a general store, purchasing hand warmers, trail mix, and other hiking supplies. Elizabeth, the oldest daughter, looked around and saw Christmas decorations scattered throughout the store. There was only one thing she didn't like about traveling for Christmas, she remarked. She missed having a Christmas tree.

Overhearing his daughter's comment, Michael disappeared into the aisles of the store. Enlisting Cody, his stepson, to keep the curious little girls distracted, he set a slight change of plans into motion.

The day of the hike arrived, and the family drove away from the city, headed for the foothills. As everyone climbed out of the car, Michael slung a backpack over his shoulders. He was to carry the water bottles and snacks they had purchased the day before. Soon they were marching through the snow, singing carols and looking for the perfect spot to stand for a photograph and a great view of Mount Rainier.

As they hiked, Michael scanned their surroundings; he was looking for something. "I think this one will do," he finally said, walking over to a small evergreen tree growing alongside the path. Six feet high and spindly, it was rather unimpressive in contrast to the other, more majestic trees that surrounded it. "Yes, it's perfect," he said, then knelt down, unzipped his backpack, and reached inside.

Not certain of what he was doing, the young girls gathered around to see what was in the backpack. To their delight, Dad pulled out a small collection of Christmas ornaments and began to decorate the tree. Within moments, it was the most beautiful tree in the forest, adorned with shiny red and silver orbs, gold tinsel, and candy canes. To finish, he hoisted Elizabeth up, and she placed a glitter-covered plastic angel on top of their Christmas tree.

As they all held hands and sang "O Christmas Tree," Michael's girls looked up at him and agreed—it was their best Christmas gift yet.

~IT'S THE LITTLE THINGS~

WHEN PAMELA STARTED having a family of her own, she found herself calling her mom quite often to ask for advice about child rearing matters. Whenever her dad answered the phone, he'd talk with her for a couple of minutes and then hand the phone over to her mom. The women would then talk for some time about the original reason for Pamela's call, but eventually the conversation turned to other events in their lives. They chatted, laughed, and ended their phone calls by saying "I love you" to each other.

Soon, Pamela realized that if her dad answered her call, he almost immediately offered to give the phone to his wife. It dawned on her that she was spending very little time talking with him. Remembering all the days of her youth when he had shown interest in her activities and made as much time for her as she wanted, she began to make phone calls home to talk only with him. If her mom answered the call, she would ask for her dad.

The first time she told her dad she had called to speak with him, she heard a lift in his voice. He was pleased when he realized she had called to ask for his advice. At first their calls were brief and to the point but quickly began to meander into other subjects and sometimes lasted nearly an hour. They talked about children, sports, hometown news, even a little bit of politics. Dad always asked Pamela if she was happy, and she answered yes, she was, especially after talking with him.

They, too, ended each conversation by saying "I love you" to each other.

It was only a phone call, but to Vincent it was a welcomed reconnection with his little girl.

Even though his daughter may be grown,
Dad still wants to be a part of her life.

~: THERE FOR HER :~

JACK WAS THE younger of two children. His father, a physician, died at the age of thirty-three. Only five years old at the time of his father's death, Jack was raised by his independent and strong-willed mother, who never married again. Jack became an equally independent and strong-willed young man.

He was also quite smart, bright enough to go to medical or law school, but he decided against those careers because he didn't want to add the financial burden of graduate school to his mother's worries. Instead, he completed an undergraduate degree and began working as a salesman for a paper company where he rose quickly through the ranks.

When Jack had children of his own, he clearly expected them to do their best in all things. Laziness was not tolerated. Lidia, his oldest, was as bright as her father, so his expectations for her were particularly high. She always seemed to meet or exceed them.

She received straight A's in numerous honors classes, sang in the school chorus, learned to play the guitar, was a skilled cheerleader, and still found time to become an accomplished ballerina. Jack was delighted with how his daughter made no waste of her intelligence and capabilities.

In the year of her high-school graduation, the honors students were brought on stage before an audience of peers and parents to be lauded for their impressive achievements. The principal announced each student's career aspiration as certificates were presented. When Lidia was called, he hesitated before announcing her aspiration; she wanted to be a choreographer.

More than any other activity she had mastered, Lidia loved to dance. Yet, wanting to please her dad, she pursued a double college major in dance and biology. It gave her options, she explained to her parents. Jack was pleased with her decision, hoping she might become the doctor he had not.

When Lidia first began to plan for graduate school, she knew her father would be disappointed that she had decided to become a university dance professor, not a doctor. Anxious, she asked her best friend to go home with her one weekend to break the news to him. Lidia positioned her friend strategically between herself and her father, hoping her friend's presence would keep her dad from overreacting, and then told him of her plans.

Jack just sat quietly and stared ahead as he listened.

When Lidia finished explaining herself, there was a long silence. She thought she was going to collapse from the tension in the air. Her best friend grabbed her hand, squeezing it tightly.

Jack finally turned his gaze toward his daughter, smiled, and then nodded and said, "Good for you, kid."

It seems that what he had wanted all along was for Lidia to follow her heart. He had chosen not to follow his own ambitions because of his mother's circumstances, but he wanted his children to freely pursue their dreams. Lidia had her dreams, and he wasn't going to stand in her way.

Lidia went on to get a master's degree in dance at Ohio State University and landed her first full-time university faculty position when she was just twenty-five years old.

Although she was a bit nervous as she began her career, she remembered her father encouraging her to never doubt her abilities. From then on, it never occurred to her that she would not succeed at dancing or teaching. To no one's surprise, she excelled at both.

Seven years ago, toxic shock ran through Lidia's veins; she fell seriously ill and plummeted into a coma. At the same time, her father, then living in California, lay in a hospital bed, being evaluated after experiencing the painful symptoms of heart disease. When Jack was finally told his daughter was in a coma in a hospital in Virginia, he promptly checked himself out of the hospital and went home to sit by the phone. He never left the house during the six days Lidia was unconscious, and he always grabbed the phone as soon as it rang.

When Lidia woke up, she could not see, walk, talk, or use her hands. Her dance and university careers were over.

During the first two years of her recovery, her dad called her every day. Before this time, Jack rarely talked on the phone, usually just grunting out a greeting before handing the phone to his wife. But now his daughter needed him in a way neither he nor she had ever expected. He became a verbose conversationalist, making Lidia talk and use her brain, challenging her to vocalize the thoughts that he believed were trapped within her mind.

Jack knew his brightest child, his first daughter, was still there, capable as ever. As had been the case once before, his expectations were high; his daughter would make no waste of her intelligence on his watch.

To the surprise of all, except perhaps her dad, Lidia eventually made a remarkable recovery.

Dads help daughters climb the mountains that are in their way.

❧ NO LIMITS ☙

HEATHER'S DAD MADE sure his only daughter found a box of chocolates on her nightstand each Valentine's Day and a beautiful corsage next to her breakfast plate every Easter Sunday; the birthday or Christmas present she wanted most was always on the top of his shopping list.

Although Joe was careful not to spoil her too much, he also did his best not to let his daughter want for anything. Memories of his own childhood, living without indoor plumbing and too many meals of fried catfish snatched from a nearby lake, drove him to give his daughter the things he'd had to live without. He simply wanted his daughter to have better memories of childhood than he had.

One Christmas Eve, Joe opened the cardboard box that held the many pieces of a bicycle Heather was to find beside the Christmas tree the next morning. As he read over the instructions and spread out the parts on the floor in the correct order of assembly, he realized several key pieces were missing from the box.

Refusing to have Heather's Christmas be short one very important gift, he packed up the bicycle parts and at two in the morning drove back to the warehouse store where he had purchased it. Undaunted by the dimmed retail signage and locked front doors, he went around to the back of the building and climbed up on the loading dock. He stood in the dark cold and pounded on the metal door for as long as it took for someone to finally open up and see what the commotion was all about.

When Heather woke up Christmas morning, she found the very bicycle she had thought of when she wrote "a new bike" on her Christmas wish list a few weeks earlier.

By the time Heather's high-school graduation neared, Joe had fallen on hard times. An ambitious entrepreneur but too generous and trusting to be a good businessman, he had by then lost several businesses.

Although Joe wanted to continue giving Heather gifts, she tried hard not to speak out loud when she daydreamed of having something new; she said no whenever asked if she needed or wanted anything. When he insisted on taking her shopping for new clothes to wear to college, she steadfastly refused to try on more than one dress. She searched through the clothing racks, settled on a modestly priced dress, and headed off for the dressing room. Moments later there was a knock at the door. When Heather peered out, she saw a saleswoman holding several other dresses. "Your dad said it will break his heart if you don't try these on," she said.

Joe managed to find ways to give Heather the things he thought she would enjoy well into her adult life, and she continued to graciously accept them, knowing each was a token of love, an expression of how much she meant to her dad.

The last gift Joe purchased in his life was a hand-knit white receiving blanket adorned with flowers and butterflies, and a matching bonnet and sweater. They were gifts for his first grand-child that unfortunately he would never see. Heather has safely stored the bonnet and sweater, but she and her daughter enjoy the blanket, both aware of how difficult it might have been for Joe to purchase such a nice gift, and both aware of how much it meant to him to be able to give it nonetheless.

A dad's generosity knows no limits
where his daughter is concerned.

⌣: SPECIAL SIGNS :⌣

ONCE AN ARTIST wannabe, I love visiting museums and galleries and have passed that on to Meagan. We have visited many exhibitions and seen some of the world's most famous paintings. We have dabbled in our own art projects, too, doing everything from clay sculptures to oil painting and creative photography. We've also spent many an evening in one of those paint-it-yourself ceramic studios, leaving with colorful plates, change holders, casserole dishes, and the like. Some of these pieces I display in our home alongside the artwork we have begun to collect.

It was to such a studio we returned a few months ago, around Father's Day, when Meagan wanted us to do something reminiscent of what we once did "back in the old days." Searching among the unfinished ceramic for the perfect piece to paint and fire, we selected two identical coffee mugs. I, a daily consumer of at least three cups, and Meagan, planning to begin drinking coffee during her college years—we decided these would become our tangible reminders of each other while we were apart. We would paint one for each other.

We sat down to our plain white mugs and discussed what to paint; it was important they matched at least a little. We finally settled on a jigsaw puzzle pattern. I planned to paint hers in pastel yellow, pink, green, and lavender, and she chose traditional military camouflage colors for mine.

We spent hours drawing and then painting the puzzle pieces on our mugs. As we worked, we talked about the events of our lives, our blended family, and her plans for the future. We laughed about the time when, during a parents-day event at school, I accidentally showed her classmates home movies of when she was a toddler and holding her dress up over her head. She thanked me for sitting beside her in the emergency room, making jokes and keeping her calm while the doctor stitched up her nearly severed finger.

When we compared our progress on the mugs, I saw that I worked a little faster than she did; I began to pace myself, dragging out each brush stroke for as long as I could. I wanted the talking to go on forever. We made four visits to the studio over the course of a week to finish those mugs.

As I was putting the final touches on Meagan's mug, I decided to add a heart in the center of one of the puzzle pieces. When she saw what I had done, she smiled. "Now when you drink from it," I said, "you'll be reminded of how much I love you." I then looked at my watch and realized I had to leave for an appointment; Meagan stayed behind to paint the final touches on my mug.

A week later she came home with the fired coffee mugs; they were beautiful, and we were proud of them. I put mine on the counter next to the coffee machine and planned to use it the next morning.

Mornings in our home are hectic; I have three women to make ready for their day and get out the door before they're late for school (Jill is a teacher). Before leaving to take Linley to school, I quickly poured a mug full of coffee and carried it with me to the car. It fit perfectly in my cup holder. I drank it all except for the last drop; it had turned cold by the time I got to the bottom of the deep mug.

With Linley safe at school, I returned home and went to the sink to rinse out the mug. I washed it and placed it upside down in the sink to drip dry. That was when I first saw it—a message Meagan had written on the bottom of the mug.

"I love you Daddy," it read.

When she came home that afternoon, I went to her and raved about the message on my mug. "Now when you drink from it," she said, "you'll be reminded of how much I love you too."

I still drink from that mug but handle it ever so carefully. It is now my favorite piece of art.

∿UNFORGETTABLE∿

ON SAMANTHA'S WEDDING day, the time came for her to walk down the aisle. Her father walked alongside, holding her as closely and tightly as he could while still being able to move. She was frightened by the inevitability of leaving the comfort and protection of her dad. She wished the moment with her hand clutching his arm would never end.

At the reception, Samantha wondered what words of wisdom her dad might whisper in her ear during their father-daughter dance. He was a kind and compassionate man, but also the strong, silent type. Many times before, they had communicated feelings more in the way they related to each other than with words; theirs was a language only they could understand.

When they finally moved onto the dance floor, just the two of them in the middle of the crowded room, no words of advice or inspiration were said. Instead, Samantha's dad simply said, "I love you, I'll always be here for you, and no matter what, you'll always be my little girl." Then he held her close and they danced, each knowing that nothing else needed to be said.

⌁SUPERMAN⌁

IN 1995 A new comet was discovered outside of Jupiter's orbit. Stewart found out when and where the comet would be visible in his area. He planned to take April, his six-year-old daughter, to see it pass through the night sky.

Hand in hand, they climbed to the top of a steep hill in the middle of town where a water tower stood. With a little time to spare, they talked as they waited for dusk to come and gazed now and then into the northwest where the comet was supposed to appear.

April looked at her dad and asked if the comet would fall out of the sky and hit the earth, maybe them there on that hill. He paused a moment, smiled, and reassured her that, no, it would not. She looked back into the twilight, feeling safe just because her dad had said that she would be.

The event itself lasted only moments, but, at least for Stewart, the memory of that night will last for years to come. Now, nearly ten years later, he still thinks about that comet and the night he shared a once-in-a-lifetime experience with his precious daughter—the evening when she, while holding his hand, looked up at him and believed that he would do anything and everything he could to protect her.

*"I look into his face and see the man
who kept me safe, gave me the answers
I needed, and loved me without limits.
I am forty-eight years old, and
I am still his little girl."*

᪥ THE BEST TEACHER ᪥

EACH NIGHT BEFORE bed, Lori grabbed a favorite book, climbed into her daddy's lap, and asked him to read it to her. He settled into the chair, opened the book, and page by page, pointing as he went, sounded out each word. Lori sounded them out, too, until eventually her dad steered her attention away from the writing and toward the colorful pictures.

As Lori grew up, the vocabulary of the books that interested her became more challenging. Soon she noticed her dad never finished reading the books she selected, and later he began to say he didn't have time to read to her at all.

One evening as she was walking toward her dad with a book, her mom pulled her aside and told her to stop asking her dad to read them to her. Lori, disappointed, insisted on knowing why.

"Your daddy can't read," her mom explained. When he was only nine years old, he was made to leave school and get a job to help support his struggling family.

Even though Lori was just a little girl, this news broke her heart. Her dad, a big, strong man, was embarrassed and couldn't admit that he was no longer able to read to her. Her dad had often reassured her that she could do almost anything she set her mind to. Motivated and determined, she made up her mind to teach him how to read. From then on, instead of asking her dad to read to her, she began reading her new favorite books to him. At first he smiled and complimented her reading skills, but later he began to ask Lori what certain words meant, and she'd tell him. Graduating from picture books to early readers and then to textbooks and novels, she pushed her dad to read.

Thanks to her help, he did learn how to read, eventually going back to school to complete his education. He insists he has Lori to thank for his diploma. It now hangs on the living-room wall for all to see.

ᗌ UNCONDITIONAL LOVE ᗧ

TO EMORY, HIS infant daughter's facial expressions were a great mystery. Was her smile a sign of joy, excitement, or the simple satisfaction of finally being able to relieve a little gas? Were her tears because of pain, fear, or overwhelming frustration that this first-time dad didn't know he had put her diapers on backwards?

"How do I know what to do to become a good dad?" he asked me.

As I thought of what to say to Emory, my mind drifted back to when Meagan was an infant. As I held my baby girl, I often imagined the things I hoped we would do together one day: ride our bicycles through the neighborhood, swim in the ocean, and lie on our backs in the grass to look for constellations in the night sky.

During her early years, we did do those things and so much more, all of which proved to be opportunities for us to nourish our attachment to each other and for me to give her all my attention and affection. The time we spent together playing also taught me about being a good dad. I learned to be more patient, to forgive messy mistakes and lost treasures, and to reassure rather than scold. I also learned how to have fun again.

Years later, the way Meagan and I spent our time together shifted from childlike play to complex tasks like helping my teenage daughter memorize the periodic table, solve algebra problems, and when she would allow, navigate her relationships with friends. Sometimes she listened carefully to what I had to say; other times she just rolled her eyes and exhaled a thinly disguised sigh of annoyance and exasperation.

It wasn't long before I realized that I, the once all-knowing and revered teacher, was on the cusp of becoming a dim-witted irritant, and my teen, a disgruntled stranger. We were headed into a difficult phase in our relationship, one I always knew was coming and would have done anything to avoid.

During that phase, Meagan learned I could lose my patience and eventually my temper, and I learned what it was like to believe that your own child really didn't like you very much anymore.

Most daughter-dad relationships become strained during adolescence, when a little girl struggles to become a young woman and a daddy struggles to let go of his little sweetheart's hand. It's a phase when neither person is perfect or without blame. Both will at one time or another say something hurtful and regrettable; both will be stubborn, if not selfish, at times.

Both will lie awake at night, worried, wondering what has happened to the other, and hoping that things will get better soon.

Meagan is now seventeen. She's an honor student, holds down a job, makes responsible decisions, and is thoughtful of others. Yet, sometimes we still have drama. Some days I can tell she wants nothing to do with me, and other days I want to snap my fingers and make her four years old again, when she marveled at everything I did, when I could do no wrong.

Thankfully, over time we have learned to be forgiving of each other's imperfection. When all the frustration has faded, we recognize the love we share is still there and growing between us. We always hug and make up, laugh at ourselves, and then return to our normal routines.

Recalling this, I told Emory to remember to show his daughter that his love cannot be diminished by whatever challenges their relationship may face—that his love is, in fact, unconditional. I promised him that she will in turn show him a rekindled affection when maturity helps her to see that daddy had the best intentions in heart and mind at the time, and that perhaps she too was a little less than perfect.

❧ NO ORDINARY DAY ☙

A FATHER OF four daughters, Paul occasionally searched through the card racks until he found one he liked, one with a photo on the front. He then purchased the card, wrote a story or poem inside about the photo, and gave it to one of his daughters on her next birthday.

In a slight twist of that tradition, his daughter Renee found a blank card she liked, one with a black-and-white photograph of a man holding a baby girl wrapped in lace and sleeping comfortably in his arms. She bought the card and gave it to her dad, asking him to write a story for her about the photo.

Moved by the image reminiscent of time spent with Renee when she was an infant, her dad warned it might take awhile to think of the perfect story to match the beautiful photo.

Seven years later, he arrived at a hospital room to find his then-thirty-two-year-old daughter holding her newborn child. His fifth grandchild was just twenty minutes old.

Paul accompanied Renee and her husband home from the hospital, and for the next five nights stayed up with his granddaughter, rocking her to sleep while her parents rested. In those quiet hours he reflected on his relationship with Renee and remembered his excitement on the day she entered his world.

He returned home inspired and finally sat down to write a poem. Three weeks later he dropped the card in the mail.

Renee reached into her mailbox and found an envelope addressed to her, written in her father's hand. She opened it and found the card she had purchased years ago; inside was a poem about the day she was born.

"My chest swells with pride and the world is a new place, because I am this little girl's daddy," was the poem's closing line.

It may have taken awhile for her dad to write it, but with tears streaming down her face, Renee knew that she held in her hand perhaps her most precious possession in the world.

⤙ THE BRIGHT SIDE ⤚

THERE ONCE WAS a time when a dad might have turned his back on his daughter if she were to become pregnant before she was married. But Myra's story shows a different side and how far we have come.

Myra, an elementary-school teacher and her father's pride and joy, was twenty-seven years old, single and pregnant. Even though she had long hoped to be a mother, she could not celebrate being pregnant. She thought she had brought shame to her conservative and very religious parents. She didn't feel like she was her daddy's little girl anymore.

She knew she was going to keep her child, and that meant she would have to face her parents and tell them of her situation.

She sat on the floor of an empty apartment, the one she was to share with the man she had hoped would become her husband, crying and waiting for her dad to arrive.

Her father finally walked through the front door and sat cross-legged on the floor across from his daughter. He knew only that she was not going to get married and thought he was there to console her about the breakup of her engagement. He reached out to brush a tear from her cheek.

Myra looked into her father's eyes; her heart raced and she braced herself. "Daddy, I'm pregnant," she managed to say through her tears. Then she waited for his reaction, certain it would not be pleasant for her.

After only a brief moment of looking into his daughter's anxious face, he began to smile. "Yes," he shouted, raising his hands into the air. "I'm going to have another grandchild!"

Myra named her son Charles, after her father, the man she admires most in the world.

"I can look her in the eyes and say,
'I did the very best I knew how for you,
no matter what anyone else thought.'"

∽IT'S NEVER TOO LATE∾

WHEN CANDIS MADE the decision to adopt a child from China, her mother planned to accompany her on the three-week trip. For more than a year, they filled out applications, interviewed with adoption professionals, and submitted to home evaluations. As the day of departure to China neared, their excitement about adding a member to their family grew.

Just two weeks before they were to leave, Candis's mother learned she had a serious medical condition and would not be permitted to travel abroad. Candis panicked; she was not prepared to make the long trip alone, much less care for her first child without the help of her mother.

That was when her mother suggested the unexpected. "Take your father," she recommended.

Her parents had been divorced nearly thirty years; Candis and her dad were not at all close. All her life they visited together no more than twice a year and spoke on the phone only a few times in between. They had always found it difficult to understand each other and foster any real feelings of affection.

Her father was the least likely person who would want to accompany her overseas on such short notice, Candis thought, and to retrieve a baby no less. Reluctantly, but in need of help, she asked him if he would go.

He agreed to go to China nearly before she had finished asking him.

It took Lee only a week to secure the necessary paperwork to travel to China; he dropped everything to make it happen. He was going to help his only daughter bring home her first child, his first granddaughter. He carried a photo around with him that had been attached to the infant girl's medical records, and he showed it to all his friends. "She's my granddaughter," he boasted.

During the three weeks they spent in China waiting for the adoption to be finalized, Candis began to get to know her dad. She discovered things about him she had never realized. She learned that he was kind, reflective, and wanted to have a better relationship with his daughter. She realized that she, too, wanted to have her dad finally be a part of her life.

The day of the adoption finally arrived and passed without a hitch. When she had signed the last form, Candis reached for the one-year-old child she had named Anna, who then promptly reached for the man sitting next to her new mom. Anna would later come to call him Pop-Pop.

Over the next several days, it was Pop-Pop who fed Anna and rocked her to sleep; it was Pop-Pop who made her laugh and smile. Anna brought out in Pop-Pop the father Candis had never seen but always wanted. As he continued to drop his guard and open his heart to his grandchild, his adult daughter's own heart began to heal. Candis, for the first time since she was a young child, began to feel a bond with her dad.

When they returned home, Pop-Pop spent several nights in Candis's home, helping his daughter and granddaughter settle in. It was the first time they had slept under the same roof since the divorce, but it seemed as familiar as if they had lived together for years. Even Candis's mom joined them; everyone celebrated the arrival of Anna.

When the time came to return to his own home, Pop-Pop said he would be back soon to see his girls. He returned the next weekend, and every weekend after that, for more than a year, even though he lived five hours away. Taking care not to miss any details of how Anna was getting along, he called Candis every night in between his weekly visits. During those calls he asked about Candis, too, and began to tell her he loved her just before he hung up the phone.

Pop-Pop passed away before Candis returned to China to adopt her second daughter; if he had not, she knows she would have asked him to go along with her to meet his second granddaughter.

Today Candis is in the early stages of her third adoption. This time she plans to bring home a son, and she has already decided to name him Lee, after her dad.

❧ SIGNS OF LOVE ❧

A WOMAN ONCE told me of how her dad and his twin brother learned to play cribbage while serving in the army during the Second World War. The brothers in turn taught their children how to play the army way, which meant cussing at crucial moments during the game.

Most nights after dinner Rachel and her father settled down to play cribbage, knowing full well mother wouldn't approve of the course language coming from their mouths during the game. In spite of getting scolded by Mom, it was a bonding experience for daughter and dad, one Rachel never forgot.

Years after her dad died, her mother asked if there was anything she wanted to take as a remembrance of her father. Rachel chose his cribbage board, and with it she has taught her own children to play the game she and her dad loved. Of course, she has taught them to play the army way.

As I listened to her story, I wondered what things of mine Meagan might keep after I'm gone and which gifts I have given her will rise to the status of treasured keepsakes. Alone in the house one afternoon, I climbed the steps to her room and took a look around.

There at the foot of her bed was the cedar chest I had refurbished for her. On her bookcase was a small ceramic statue of a cow I had painted during one of our daddy-daughter dates, complete with a gold bracelet above one hoof and blue stud earrings in both ears. Above her desk was displayed a partially finished still-life oil painting we had started years ago but never finished. On her walls were photographs I had taken. On her bulletin board were old notes I'd left on her dashboard or hidden in a school textbook.

At her age now, she doesn't readily tell me how she feels about me, but I've learned that if I keep my eyes open, I eventually find out. I see sweet evidence that tells me that even though at times she doesn't want me near, she holds me close nonetheless.

*"We always seem to know what
each other is thinking."*

‿∴SUBTLE LESSONS∾

JASON AND YVETTE were working hard to save money for their young family, and with thrift in mind, Yvette asked her husband not to purchase anything for her for the approaching Valentine Day. Although Jason would have liked to give his wife a gift, he respected her wishes and refrained from sending flowers to her office or hiding a box of chocolates in her briefcase.

Valentine Day passed without ceremony for Yvette—almost.

When she arrived at the preschool to pick up their daughter, Yvette found her two-year-old holding a single red rose and a red balloon. Jason had visited the preschool earlier in the day and delivered a Valentine Day gift to his beloved little girl.

Later at home, Yvette asked Jason about his gift to their child. He told her he wanted his daughter to know from the very beginning how a man should treat her. "If a man can't treat her as well as or better than her daddy, then she needn't be bothered with him," he said.

What a great lesson for a young girl to learn, and what better person to teach it than her daddy, Yvette thought as she nodded.

That day, seeing how well her husband treated their child and the smile on her face as she proudly held up the rose and balloon for Mommy to see were the best Valentine Day gifts Yvette could ever hope for.

⌁ SUPPORT THAT NEVER WAVERS ⌁

TWENTY-FIVE YEARS ago, Susan became the first person in her family to attend college. In some ways her parents didn't quite know what to make of her desire to continue her education beyond high school. After all, her dad left school after the third grade, and her mother, the eighth grade, and both were doing just fine.

In spite of her parents' reservations, Susan immersed herself in her college education, initially commuting to classes from home. By the end of the first semester, she had made many new friends and was discovering an exhilarating world, one that existed out from under the watch of her parents. As the next semester approached, she decided to leave home for on-campus living and the chance to spread her wings even further.

Her parents, unable to contribute more to the cost of their daughter's education, advised that if she felt independent enough to leave home, she was independent enough to get a job to pay her dormitory expenses. Susan secured an on-campus job that paid well enough to cover the cost of her room but not the campus meal plan. Determined not to ask her parents for additional help, she sustained herself eating peanut-butter sandwiches at nearly every meal, sitting alone on the bed in her dorm.

Dad eventually found out about his daughter's sandwich diet. Instead of seizing upon that knowledge as an excuse to encourage her to move back home, he began stopping by the dorm on surprise visits to see her, coincidentally, just in time to ask her to join him for dinner. More than once, he insisted they drive to the restaurant in her old car, only to stop at a gas station so he could fill the tank. Some nights when he dropped her off back at the dorm, he slipped a little cash into her hand as she hugged him good-bye for the evening.

Susan finished college with a degree in fabric arts and has made a comfortable living for herself as a fabric designer and art instructor. She no longer needs to get by on peanut-butter sandwiches, but she knows she might not have gotten so far if not for her dad and his surprise visits to her dorm room.

"He never fails to tell me what a great person I have grown up to be. I, in turn, tell him that I am who I am because of the great father he has always been."

◡⬝ EASY TO PLEASE ⬝◡

MUCH OF MY former corporate career was spent working for small start-up companies. A few succeeded; many failed. Consequently, if you were to chart my annual income on a line graph, it would resemble an EKG of someone in full cardiac arrest.

When Meagan was ten years old, I was having a particularly bad year and doing everything I could think of to minimize our cost of living. We had turned to watching more television and playing board games instead of indulging in outings that included a price of admission. One evening while playing dominoes on the floor in front of the television, I broke some bad news.

"I'm not sure I can afford to take us on a vacation this summer," I said.

"I don't care," she responded quickly. "We don't have to go anywhere; I just want us to be together."

I was pleasantly surprised by her response. My little girl wasn't upset that a cruise or theme-park vacation package wasn't in her near future. Instead of being disappointed in me, she was reassuring me that I had not disappointed her.

I suddenly became determined to find a way to do something

fun and exciting for her even if it had to be a one-day vacation.

As the evening wore on, we switched channels, trying to find something entertaining to watch. We settled on a food program featuring the famous restaurants of Chicago and learned of Eli's, a place known for its version of Meagan's favorite dessert, cheesecake.

"Maybe we can go there one day," she said.

On Friday night a week later, I asked her to go to bed early; we were getting up in the wee hours of the next morning to fly to Chicago, I explained. I had cashed in all my frequent-flyer points, and we were going to eat cheesecake at Eli's. Even if it would only be for a day, we were going on vacation.

We made the most of our day in Chicago—we ate deep-dish pizza for lunch, visited the Art Institute of Chicago and the observation deck of the Hancock Center, rode the Ferris wheel at Navy Pier, and laughed our heads off as we were splashed with water while taking a speedboat ride on Lake Michigan.

Before heading back to the airport for our flight home, we stopped at Eli's. You'll never be able to convince Meagan and me that our dessert was anything less than the best cheesecake ever made.

Exhausted from our day of fun, Meagan fell asleep leaning against my chest during the flight home but not before telling me how much she had enjoyed our vacation.

We've been on a number of vacations since then, visiting

some fabulous places, seeing famous landmarks and searching for celebrities, but Meagan still calls that day in Chicago her favorite vacation. She can't even imagine how happy that makes me. It was one of my favorite vacations too.

"When my father and I ate ice cream, we made sure our faces showed it. Mom always mumbled, 'Not again,' as she cleaned me up, and I could hear Dad laughing in the background."

⌇LOVE HEALS⌇

GLENDA GREW UP knowing her father loved her, but his withdrawn and gruff nature made it such that she didn't always feel that love.

Being the kind of dad who was often in a bad mood after coming home from work, what he wanted to do most was have dinner and then relax watching television. Glenda knew that he worked hard and was tired at the end of the day, but she needed more from him than she was getting. Their relationship was strained even in its best moments.

Everything about their relationship changed in a way Glenda couldn't have imagined the evening she came home with her boyfriend and told her parents she was pregnant.

Expecting her dad to go into a rage before kicking her out of the house, she braced herself. Instead, he looked at her and calmly said, "Whether it is a boy or a girl, I expect you to name the baby after me."

His name was Fuston. When his own father was born, his name was supposed to be Houston, but the doctor who delivered him was drunk and wrote Fuston on the birth certificate by mistake. The name stuck and was passed down to Glenda's dad.

Fuston stood, reached for his daughter, and hugged her.

From that point forward, he became the dad she had always wanted. He accompanied Glenda to all her prenatal appointments and provided her with financial support and, more importantly, abundant emotional support. His loving attention and protection began to fill the void she had endured all the previous years.

When his granddaughter, Sadie, was born and her father was nowhere to be found, it was Fuston who abruptly retired and became Glenda's nanny, cook, and housekeeper. Her dad, the man who always disappointed her as a child, was now the one who lifted her spirits and kept her going. All those years of hurt were healed in a matter of months as he showed her every day how much he loved her.

When Sadie was a toddler, her grandparents had to move to another state. Glenda stayed behind with her child and set out to make it on her own. In the beginning she didn't have a telephone or cable or antennae for her television. Fuston taped her favorite shows and sent them by mail each week, along with prepaid calling cards and other goodies in an overstuffed care package.

A few years later, Glenda's parents decided to move back to be nearer to their grandchild. During the move, Fuston injured himself, and while he was being treated, it was discovered he was in the final stages of cancer. He died only five months later.

Glenda feels her father's absence every day, but she also finds comfort in remembering that when she needed him the most, he was there for her after all.

Sadie is now fourteen years old. When Sadie is moody or does something that reminds Glenda of her dad, she calls her daughter "Fustonette" just as her dad had asked her to.

A dad's loving-kindness heals
any wounds his shortcomings
and misunderstandings may make.

⋰AFFECTIONATE GESTURES⋱

SAFELY TUCKED AWAY in Jill's desk drawer is an old photograph of her, one taken when she was nine years old. She's sitting on her bed, grinning broadly and holding a stuffed animal, Benji the dog.

When I first saw the photograph, I couldn't help but laugh, seeing my wife at such a young age before braces had narrowed the gaps between her teeth, her curly red hair in careless bangs, and wearing a blouse sporting a frilly Peter Pan collar.

She immediately snatched the photo from my hand and, gazing longingly at Benji, admonished me for laughing at her.

It turns out that stuffed animal is one of her most prized possessions. Her dad had given it to her.

Johnny, an electrical engineer, worked long hours at an airplane-manufacturing plant. His wife, a part-time teacher, did most of the shopping errands for the family, including selecting all the birthday and Christmas presents. Johnny's role in the gift-giving process was simply to sign the card and then watch as his two children unwrapped their presents.

The movie *Benji* was on theater screens then, and like most children in America in 1974, Jill adored the lead character.

Johnny knew this, and one day as he walked through a department store in search of new white shirts to wear to work, he impulsively grabbed a stuffed Benji from a display as he passed.

Returning home, he walked into Jill's room and announced he had brought home a surprise for her. Jill reached for the department-store bag, somewhat in disbelief that her father, the man she believed didn't know where the grocery store was, had actually gone shopping. When she looked inside and saw Benji, she was thrilled, not only to have the stuffed animal, but because her dad had thought of her during the day. He had purchased the perfect gift for her, without any help from Mom.

Jill slept with Benji until she left home to attend college nine years later.

I asked about Benji one afternoon while Jill and I were having lunch with my in-laws. As my mother-in-law told me he was stored in a box on a shelf in a closet, I looked over at my wife. She and her dad were looking at each other across the table and smiling. Not a word was spoken between them, yet their expressions said plenty.

Some memories never fade.

⌒BRING OUT THE BEST⌒

SILVIA'S FATHER, BENJAMIN, is a single dad who raised three children, including two daughters, mostly by himself with the occasional support of his mother. From an early age, Silvia understood that her dad was not very expressive. He was neither physically affectionate nor verbally reassuring to his children. He believed that working hard to provide for his children, making an appearance at their school events, and offering the coveted birthday or Christmas gift were plenty evidence of his love. Otherwise, he remained distant, especially from his daughters. He never told them, "I love you," or, "You're beautiful."

Until she was fourteen years old, Silvia relied on her grandmother for the emotional nurturing she could not get from her dad. When her grandmother passed away, Silvia lost her best friend and the only adult she thought truly loved her.

Even though her grandmother had tried to help her understand her dad, Silvia felt unloved and unwanted instead of treasured by her father. Watching her friends' affectionate interplay with their fathers left her hurt and jealous, and eventually angry. She began to relate to her dad as he had related to her for years, from a quiet, silent distance.

She left home to go to college, one intentionally far away from home, telling herself she would not return to visit her father. He didn't much care about her anyway, she reasoned. He wouldn't be the man who would walk her down the aisle when her wedding day came, either.

They did not speak much for nearly two years, and when they did, conversation was cordial at best, but never very warm.

One day Silvia recalled a pastor's message about hope and love, one delivered to her years earlier when her grandmother was slipping away. The hard-to-love needed to be loved, he had said. Then and there, she became determined to love her nearly unlovable dad. She remembered the daughter-dad relationships she had watched in high school, but this time instead of being overcome with jealousy, she found inspiration. She saw the possibility of what she could have with her dad, but she knew she was going to have to work for it.

The following weekend Silvia walked into her dad's house. As soon as the opportunity arose, she clung to him—and wouldn't let go. "I need you to tell me you love me," she said.

"You know I do," he answered.

"I need you to say it, Dad. Tell me you love me."

With her arms still clinched around his waist, he looked into her eyes and saw how earnest she was. Finally, although somewhat awkwardly, he told his daughter what she wanted to hear. "I love you, Silvia."

"I love you, too, Dad," she said, smiling and pressing her face against his chest over his heart.

That moment was the new beginning for their relationship.

Although changes occurred slowly, Silvia refused to let her dad fall back into his unaffectionate, unexpressive comfort zone. She pushed him again and again, requiring him to initiate interaction with her, reminding him she wanted to hear the thoughts that dwelled in his heart. She told him she wanted him to hug her first once in a while.

Slowly, Benjamin began to understand how he needed to interact with his daughter. Slowly but deliberately, he began to reach out to her. Soon, he began to call Silvia at college, at first only after her visits home to make sure she had returned to her apartment safely, and later, to find out when she was coming back to see him again.

Today Silvia is twenty-three years old and about to be married. From the first moment she became engaged, she knew that it would be her dad who would walk her down the aisle on her wedding day.

❦ BEST INTENTIONS ❧

JOYCE'S FATHER HAD been teaching her right from wrong since she was a little girl. She admired his wisdom and always took his lessons to heart. When she became a teen, however, her adherence to his advice began to slip.

She began dating in high school and found she enjoyed dating several boys at the same time instead of going steady with just one suitor. More than once, she had two dates on the same day and only grinned when her dad warned she was playing a dangerous game. Joyce continued playing that game in college, juggling several boyfriends and staying out until the early hours of the morning. Dad's warnings and pleadings now fell on deaf ears.

One summer Joyce worked as a resident assistant in her campus dormitory. She was also dating a fellow student, someone her father was not very fond of. When she called home and asked him to bring her a cooler she needed for a group picnic, he obliged. It was a chance to check up on her.

When he arrived on campus, he found a group of students packing their cars with food, blankets and towels, Frisbees, and other things college students would take to the lake on a sunny afternoon. As Dad reached into the car trunk to lift out the ice-filled cooler, a young man approached him, shook his hand vigorously when he introduced himself as Anthony, and proceeded to help carry the cooler.

Impressed, Dad whispered to his daughter, "Why not a guy like that? Good looking, a great smile, and a no-nonsense handshake." Joyce told her dad to mind his own business, but as the day wore on, she kept finding herself watching Anthony.

Joyce and Anthony soon began dating and then one day discovered they were going to have a baby. Upon hearing the news, Anthony dropped to his knee in Joyce's dorm room and asked her to become his bride. She said yes.

They drove to her parents' home to break the news. Sitting across from the parents in the living room, Anthony cautiously explained their situation and announced their plans to marry.

Dad leaned forward, faced the young man he had advised his daughter to date, and in a deep growl warned, "If you ever hurt my little girl, you'll wish you never came into our lives."

Anthony, without missing a beat, responded, "I assure you, sir, I will never hurt your daughter. I love her." With that Anthony reached out and shook his future father-in-law's hand with the same determination to impress him as when they first met. Joyce and Anthony married, and the following late summer they presented her dad with a baby boy, his first grandchild.

Today, the couple is looking forward to celebrating their twenty-eighth wedding anniversary, and Joyce is once again thankful she finally began to listen to her dad's advice.

﹌NEVER TOO BIG﹏

EARLY ONE SPRING a few years ago, I found myself taking family photographs on a farm in Ohio. A young teen daughter loved riding on her dad's back, even though she was almost too big for him to carry easily. Watching the dad try to hold her still for the photo reminded me of Meagan when she was young and loved to cling to me.

In the beginning, I would kneel and hold her sitting in the palm of my hand, balancing her as she kicked and squealed. A few pounds later, she sat on my foot, wrapped her arms around my leg, and rode along as I walked through the house. When she became too big for that, she graduated to riding on my shoulders and then eventually to my back.

I remember one afternoon when she was five or six, I carried her on my back as I climbed up the steep incline of Stone Mountain, just under a one-and-a-half-mile trek. Back then I was glad she was getting too big for such things. I didn't want this back-ride up the mountain to become a regular event.

Now, nearly a dozen years later, I wish I could still do it.

Approaching fifty, I worry for the first time about how much strength and ability I will eventually lose to age. Not because I'm necessarily afraid of growing old, but because I don't want to be less able to do things for my girls. They call on me to carry their luggage upstairs, hoist heavy boxes of packed-away keepsakes into the attic, or give them the occasional piggyback ride across a parking lot. These are the things a dad does, and it saddens me to think that one day I may not be able to do any of them.

A few months ago, I was in a swimming pool with Meagan and Linley when both dared me to pick them up on my shoulders. Teasing me and calling me an old man, Linley was certain I couldn't lift two teens into the air. It was a challenge I could not ignore.

After squatting down underwater for so long my eyes bulged from my need to breathe, the girls finally got positioned, one on each shoulder. My feet planted firmly on the pool floor, and while holding them by their knees, I rose up, lifting them into the air. It lasted only a moment, just long enough for Jill to get a photo of the girls ripping my hair out as they fell back into the water.

It lasted only a moment, but I did it.

❧ THE TABLES WILL TURN ❧

STANDING IN THE KITCHEN with her mother, peeling potatoes, Andrea looked into the den at her dad. He sat quietly in a recliner, slouching a little and watching television with her two little girls. Her parents had come to visit for the weekend to see their granddaughters.

She saw that her dad moved slowly, his shoulders no longer strong and square, and his knuckles now thickened and stiff with arthritis. Age had not been kind to him, she realized; he could no longer do as much as he once did.

She remembered when he was strong and industrious, working hard nearly every day, even sometimes on Sundays and holidays. After a long shift at the textile mill, he came home for supper, did the things around their house that needed his attention, and then went to his parents' home to help them care for their farm.

As busy as he was, though, he always made time for Andrea, doing what he could to fulfill her childhood requests. When she wanted a soapbox go-cart, he made one from scrap wood and spare parts. When she wanted a skateboard, he made one, again from scrap wood and spare parts. Because she dreamed of becoming a gymnast, he erected parallel bars in the backyard so she could practice as much as she wanted to. He made a seesaw under the shade tree in their backyard and rode it with her. He was never too busy, sore, or tired to play with his only child.

Saddened that her once-capable father was now limited, Andrea mourned for the times years ago when she was convinced he could do anything, because in her eyes he usually did. It wasn't fair that he couldn't play with his grandchildren as much as they wanted him to. He should have that simple reward after how much he had worked to help so many others all his life, she thought.

Her daughters, by then bored with watching television, left the room, only to return to their grandfather's side with a bag of marbles. "Play with us," they begged. He, unwilling to deny anything they requested of him, slowly and carefully rose from the recliner and lowered himself to the floor. Once seated, a granddaughter flanking each side, he proceeded to teach them how to shoot marbles.

Andrea saw a familiar twinkle in his eyes as he leaned toward the floor and explained how to aim, and she imagined that just maybe he still could do anything. Even if he could not, she decided as she watched her daughters laughing while trying to flick the marbles, it wouldn't matter. Now it was her time to do anything for him.

Daughters never forget
what their dads have done for them.

❧

◡·ALL YOU NEED IS TIME·◞

MY NEIGHBOR, PETER, and his eight-year-old daughter, Lucy, have a close relationship founded on many special moments he has created for his firstborn. Together they enjoy a Donut Friday breakfast tradition before he drops her off at school. He reads to her each night before she goes to bed, brings her a new snow globe after every business trip (she now has forty-two), and creates adventure stories and biographies for all her stuffed animals.

Lucy is especially delighted when her dad takes time away from work to participate in her Indian Princess activities. He even thought up Lucy's Indian name, River Willow, apt because she likes water and willow trees. Dad's Indian name is Yellow Snow, for reasons Lucy doesn't yet understand.

One fall weekend, they attended an overnight Indian camping adventure. Peter had managed to adjust his calendar even though he learned of the camping trip just two days before the scheduled departure. During the drive to the camp, Lucy, learning how to read a map, served as navigator. It was a coed weekend, and Lucy fretted about how well the Indian Braves would treat the Indian Princesses.

The young boys and girls actually got along quite well during the first day, competing against one another in field events, but that all changed as the sun went down. Under the cover of shadows, the boys invaded the girls' cabin and tried to scare them with Silly String and rubber snakes and bugs. In swift retaliation, one daughter's dad made a hurried visit to a nearby bait shop and returned to camp with over one hundred live crickets. As the moon shined bright, the crickets were stealthily released inside the boys' cabin.

That night the Indian Princesses slept well; the Indian Braves, not so well.

I asked Lucy what she admired most about her dad. Her answer was immediate and sincere: "I like it that he spends so much time with me."

"Dad didn't know anything more than any other new dad on the block, but he gave parenting his best shot and worked hard to be good at it."

❧ LASTING MEMORIES ❧

ON A RECENT family vacation, Noelle's dad, Vernon, took everyone to Alaska. While they were exploring Juno, he said he wanted to buy her a nice piece of jewelry. After searching through a number of stores, she found a small loose diamond she thought would make a perfect necklace. They paid for it and were told it would be ready for pickup in two hours.

As they left the jewelry store, Vernon suddenly remembered they had theater tickets for a show he really wanted to see. It was scheduled to begin at the same time they were to pick up the necklace. If they didn't get the diamond necklace that afternoon, they wouldn't be able to return to the store before needing to leave for home. He told Noelle not to worry and reassured her they could get to the jewelry store and still make it to the theater on time.

Unfortunately, two hours later it started to rain, and worse, they missed the bus into town. With no cabs in sight, they shrugged and walked in their best shoes and outfits through the rain and mud to get the necklace. Vernon never complained, pulling his daughter along with him through the town of Juno and doing his best to protect her from rain and puddles. Soaked, they finally arrived at the jewelry store.

They hurriedly picked up the necklace, the most beautiful piece of jewelry Noelle had ever owned, and then ran to the theater. They made it to their seats with barely a minute to spare and chuckled at each other as they blotted their wet hair with napkins he had grabbed on the way in. They were still damp and winded when the curtain went up. Noelle looked over at her dad's face, and he beamed when the first entertainer walked out onto the stage.

When Noelle thinks of that summer vacation in Alaska, she does not dwell on the diamond necklace her dad had made for her and which she still wears from time to time. Instead, she remembers how far he would go, and what he would do without, just to make her happy. And, of course, she remembers that smile on his face.

*A daughter remembers
how well Dad treated her long after
she has forgotten what things he gave her.*

❧ GIFT OF LOVE ❧

JILL AND I each brought to our marriage a daughter from a previous marriage. We had a number of concerns about combining our families. After all, each girl, then ten and fourteen, had lived all her life as an only child.

Both girls had their own expectations, which they expressed without reservation, about what parent-child traditions would remain in place or be replaced and who would get the bigger bedroom or the final say in the sibling disputes they were certain would occur.

Jill and I braced ourselves on the day we moved into our new house together. We hoped for the best and prayed we could survive the worst of our fears.

At one time or another, each daughter cried tears of frustration about something the other had done or said, and there were times when each child would pull aside her parent and complain about how their relationship had changed since the marriage. But Jill and I stood firm, united as a couple and expecting our children to work out their differences and frustrations for the benefit of our newly blended family. We were determined not to be two families under one roof.

In addition to our own new family, we also concerned ourselves with our children's other blended families—both ex-spouses had remarried. In our house, providing nurture to our blended family means making sure the girls are encouraged to love and have fun with their other parents and stepparents. Jill and I want to give them a life enriched by two families.

Meagan went to a formal dance recently, and I was the appointed photographer at the before-party. Five young couples were there, all decked out in dresses and tuxedos and eagerly awaiting their limo. Meagan acted a little embarrassed as I posed her friends and snapped photos, but she was pleased with me at the same time, happy everyone wanted to have pictures taken. I took a hundred photos, and eventually we sent our kids off for the big date night.

Once back home, I downloaded the images and scanned them quickly, looking to make sure I had a few good ones of each couple. My attention suddenly went to one photograph in particular, one I forgot had been taken. Meagan's mom took it with my camera. It was of my child with her arms wrapped around my new wife and me, all three of us grinning wide.

It made me smile to see the three of us looking so happy together. It made me even happier to recall that my ex-wife took the picture and that she, Jill, and I could be together enjoying an event in Meagan's life. We were making sure Meagan could relax and enjoy herself without being stressed out in what could have been an uncomfortable situation. It is a gift of love we *all* give to her.

❄ GENTLE WORDS ❄

EVEN THOUGH NOW in her early forties, Fairlie still considers herself a daddy's little girl. She also calls herself an "oops," because she was the last child born into the family, more than a dozen years after her next nearest-in-age sibling.

Who knows if it was because she was the youngest child, the only daughter, or in her father's mind his miracle baby, but whatever the reason, Fairlie was her father's pride and joy.

An appliance salesman known to all as Sonny, he went to work several hours later in the morning than his wife did, leaving him and Fairlie a few hours of private time to enjoy each day. She began her mornings watching her dad get ready. Standing at his feet and watching him shave, comb his hair, and brush his teeth, five-year-old Fairlie thought her dad was the most handsome man in the world when he emerged from the bathroom.

Their morning activities included a walk through the neighborhood to exercise the family dog, Willie. Daughter and dad walked hand in hand, talking about whatever was on their minds and allowing Willie to lead them wherever he wished. After the walk, Fairlie was taken to her baby-sitter and would not see her dad again until late in the evening, long after the dinner dishes had been put away. Yet, no matter how many hours

Sonny worked each day, the first thing he did upon returning home was find his daughter and give her a kiss. If she had already gone to bed, she kept herself awake so she wouldn't miss his kiss and the fun of having him tuck her back into bed.

Fairlie's memories of having fun with her dad are over thirty years old; Sonny died when she was only ten. She now keeps photographs of him in her wallet and scattered around her house to remind her of their times together. Although most of her memories are as crystal-clear as if she were watching a video, she admits she had forgotten one thing about her dad— the sound of his voice.

That changed two years ago with her brother's chance discovery of a box of cassette tapes.

Sonny liked to keep in touch with his father but preferred to send him tape recordings rather than letters. He carried a cassette recorder with him everywhere he went, documenting his activities and conversations to share later with his dad and other family members. He even recorded himself "singing" with Willie, who did his best to follow along and howl in the right key.

One day Fairlie received a CD in the mail; it was simply labeled "Dad." As she played it, she heard her father's voice for the first time in nearly twenty-eight years. It was from a time when he was driving the family to a vacation spot and recorded their conversations in the car. In addition to his usual jokes and banter, she heard him explaining why they had not brought Willie along on the vacation.

Now the sound of her dad's voice, too, is as crystal-clear in her mind as are the images of them walking together, trying to keep up with Willie. And just as they always had, his words spoken that day in the car, gentle reassurances and phrases of affection, told of just how much he loved her.

Dads make daughters feel loved
in ways that no one else can.

⌁:BELOVED ROLE MODEL:⌁

BRENDA LOVED TO watch her dad, Gordon, a hard-working man who managed to support his family as a career house painter. A true craftsman, he always did his best work on each project, never skimping on details or in places the homeowner would never see.

From him she learned to work hard no matter what. If she were going to do anything, she should do it well.

As a young child, she often stood in the backyard and watched her dad gather his cans of paint, brushes, drop sheets, and ladders and load it all into his pickup truck. Always looking forward to his day of work, he whistled tunes from the Second World War era as he repeated this routine six days a week.

Brenda knew when her dad was coming home for lunch because she could hear his whistle as he walked up and reached for the handle of the screen door. At the end of most days, she watched for him from the kitchen window, waiting patiently for his return. When he finally made his appearance, he was covered in colorful droplets and smelled of paint, but was as handsome as ever to her.

One summer many years later, Gordon inspected the exterior of Brenda's home and announced he intended to paint it for her.

By that time, he was seventy-eight years old. He also announced it would be his last season working as a house painter.

Brenda, a fine-art photographer and darkroom developer, had for some time wanted to document in photos her dad at work, concentrating on his craft, brush in hand. It had not been an easy project. He discouraged her from showing up at his customers' homes with her camera gear, saying, "You can't just walk around someone's house taking pictures," or, "Posing for you will slow me down."

Undaunted, she would try to photograph familiar scenes—her dad mixing paint in his backyard and loading ladders into his truck. Stubborn, he only rose earlier, completed his preparations, and left for work before Brenda could arrive.

Gordon successfully evaded her camera for two years. But now, Brenda thought, he was painting her house; she was the customer. She would finally get the chance to take the photographs she wanted.

One early morning in August, Gordon arrived with his ladders and paint supplies, once again whistling his favorite tunes. Without delay, he went to work, scraping off old paint and sanding the clapboards of the house. Before long, Brenda discovered that trying to take photographs of her dad, even while he painted her own house, was just as difficult as it had always been. Moving relentlessly, he seldom paused to look toward the camera. He had a job to do, he said.

Over the next ten days, Brenda chased her dad around the house, dodging paint spatter, trying to catch him in just the right light and activity to depict in photographs the character of a career house painter and the man she loved—her father, her teacher. Little did she know these days would be her last opportunity to document her father's work.

Standing high on the ladder for extended periods was taking a toll on Gordon; he became dizzy and felt a stabbing pain in his side. Despite these discomforts, he pushed ahead. He was accustomed to hurdles and had courageously jumped over them, previously surviving two heart attacks and two bouts with cancer. His desire to paint his daughter's house at the close of his career provided him with the endurance he needed to finish what he had started.

Two weeks after he finished painting Brenda's house, he found himself no longer able to go to work. For the first time in over fifty years, he cancelled his remaining scheduled paint jobs.

A few days later, he learned he was battling a third cancer; he was told he had only a few months to live. Thereafter, Brenda, a mother of three, saw her father nearly every day for ten weeks. She attended to all the necessary matters that come as death nears and escorted him to all his medical appointments. She was with him when he was moved into a hospice center to await the looming inevitable.

And once more she used her camera to capture images, tender moments, of her dad as he was surrounded by those who loved him. When they were alone again, they talked, and he opened his heart in a way he never had before.

Two weeks after moving into the center, Gordon passed away, but not before he and Brenda had the chance to look through the photographs she had taken. As they looked at the last one, he said he was pleased with her work.

One year after her father's death, Brenda put the photographs on display. Like her dad, she approached her work by hand, paying attention to the finest of details, developing new prints in her own darkroom, adjusting the images until they were perfect and the spirit of her father shined through each one.

Prior to the opening of her show, she asked one of her dad's friends to whistle a few wartime songs as she recorded him. Then she recorded the sounds of a ladder being extended and as it thumped when being placed against a wall, and the sound of metal on wood as old paint was scraped from clapboard siding.

When the gallery opened, twenty black-and-white photographs representing Gordon's life graced the walls, ranging from his painting truck to the last photograph Brenda took of herself with him in his final days.

In a corner of the gallery lay one of Gordon's paint-covered drop cloths, and on it were his paint-covered work shoes, an empty paint can, and a collection of brushes and scrapers, all in the shadow of his ladder that leaned against the wall. Tools, they were, but to Brenda they were more than that. They were the symbols of a man who took pride in what he did, who believed in giving everything his best effort, and who never tired of providing for his family, no matter how hard he had to labor.

Brenda stood in the gallery, wearing his last, spatter-covered painting cap, listening to the recording she had made, and looking into the loving eyes of her dad, her role model, as the familiar sound of whistling reached her ears.

❧ QUIET INSPIRATION ☙

ONCE WHEN CAROL was a child, she walked into her parents' bedroom to say good night and found her father on his knees in prayer.

Her dad, Superman, the fellow who could handle anything and seemingly always had, was praying for guidance, forgiveness, and blessings for his family. Awestruck, Carol understood her father was humbling himself and asking for help, admitting he could not handle everything by himself after all.

The image of her beloved father acknowledging his fallibility made her aware of her own and her need for God in her life too.

"Dad gave me the motto 'Do your best, and God will do the rest.' He was right."

↶ SPECIAL BOND ↷

MEAGAN USED TO go to work with me when she wasn't in school. She was my summer travel partner, boarding airplanes like a seasoned pro, jumping on the hotel beds, and somehow always managing to convince me we needed to order breakfast from room service.

She carried her own briefcase with her when we went to work, one filled with crayons, stickers, rubber stamps and ink pads, Post-its, and other messy stuff. You could always tell where she'd been—she left tracks everywhere.

Meagan is hardly the only daughter to regularly accompany her dad to work. Stephanie rode the train into the city with her father to get to his office. To pass the time while waiting for the train, they entertained themselves playing the Name Game.

To play the Name Game, one must take a name and restate it as many times as you can in random, rhyming singsong words, as in "Stefanee, Stefanee, bo befanee, banana fanna fo fefanee, me my oh mefanee, yo Stefanee."

One morning her dad wanted to play the Name Game and told her to use the name Chuck. She promptly began singing. "Chuck, Chuck bo buck, banana fanna fo . . ." You get the picture.

Realizing what she had said, Stephanie began to cry. She looked at her dad and found him rocking in his seat, laughing so hard he was shaking. When he could talk again, he assured her it was okay that she had said that word, and he encouraged her to sing it one more time, but not before making her promise not to tell her mom.

Her story reminded me of a game Meagan and I used to play on the way to work or anytime we were stuck sitting in the car. We called it the Bucket Game. The idea was to try to gross each other out by calling each other the vilest description of whatever putrid and disgusting matter we could think of, in a bucket. As in, "You're a bucket of greasy, grimy, rotten gopher guts crawling with maggots and stinking like pig poop on a hot summer day." We could go on and on like this for miles.

I had a bad habit at the time of using a few choice words, usually describing body parts in unflattering ways, to share my thoughts about other people's driving skills during rush hour. It did not occur to me, although it should have, that my young and impressionable passenger was listening carefully and adding these words to her Bucket Game vocabulary.

One day while attending a meeting with my employees, I spied Meagan playing with the magnets on the staff scheduling board. "Stop that, you little booger," I said.

Without missing a beat she looked at me and said, "If I'm a booger, you're a bucket of . . ." I was unable to restore order in the meeting after that.

I'm not sure if Meagan learned anything from this event, and of course she didn't get in trouble for it because she didn't know any better. I, on the other hand, learned a lot, as in to be careful what I say when around my child.

Every once in a while Meagan calls me at my desk over the garage. As I answer the phone, I hear her winding up: "You're a bucket of . . ."

It is a conversation that may seem silly or gross to others, but it is always precious to me.

"When you look at my life, it's obvious I have his stubbornness, his compassionate heart, his silly sense of humor, and his positive yet realistic outlook on life. I'm proud to be my daddy's daughter."

❧ DELAYED REWARDS ❧

NOW AND THEN a daughter has the opportunity to be with her dad during his final moments. Somehow sensing when the time of departure draws near, she may stay by her dad's side, giving him comfort and care, embracing their last opportunity to exchange affectionate touches and words of love.

It was during such a time that Eleanor was with her dad. He, unable to speak, communicated with her by blinking his eyes. Three blinks meant, "I love you." She will always remember the last time he blinked that message to her, his beautiful green eyes looking so intensely into hers.

That night she fell asleep in the chair alongside his hospital bed, her head on a pillow resting next to his. Her hand was on his arm, seizing every opportunity she could to be a little closer to her dad, one more time.

Sometime during the night Eleanor's father died.

We cannot know if he was aware of his daughter's presence during his final moments, but that wasn't the point of her vigil. He had always been there for her, and that evening, *she* was there for him.

⌁ FORGIVENESS ⌁

LAST SUMMER I took the family to vacation in Key West, Florida. One day was devoted to snorkeling over the live coral reef a few miles offshore; a catamaran would take us there.

We had to arrive at the marina on time that morning or be left behind. The captain waited for no one, we had been warned. As anticipated, Meagan was running late, and as expected, I was fuming about it. Jill and Linley did their best to stay out of the way while Meagan and I traded sharp exchanges about the virtues of punctuality. We did make it onboard the catamaran in time but not without some final wailing and gnashing of teeth between Meagan and me as we took our places.

A little more than an hour later, and after most of our angst had passed, we donned our masks and flippers and jumped into the waters of the Gulf of Mexico. It was a windy day with choppy seas, making it a challenge to peacefully float above the marine life that swam some twenty feet below the surface. The current kept pushing Meagan back toward the catamaran; she couldn't keep her place over where the fish were. Tired and frustrated, she took off her mask; she was about to give up on the adventure and climb back onboard.

I swam to her side and extended my hand, and, taking hers in mine, I pulled her along with me toward the reef. Together we swam against the current, skirting between the fingers of the coral, looking for fish. Shortly we were pointing out neon blue parrot fish, yellowtail snapper, grouper, and pompanos. We were having fun.

I looked toward my daughter to see if she wanted to go farther up the reef. She nodded yes, and then I saw that her eyes sparkled behind her mask. There was a smile on her lips, too, even as she clamped down tight on her snorkel.

I noticed something else. My daughter, the one who now too rarely sits on my lap or kisses me good night, who earlier in the morning thought I was an unreasonable, overbearing troll, was still holding my hand. She had not pulled away even for a second.

Me? I was happy giving her comfort there in the middle of the ocean. I was doing what I love to do, taking care of my kid. I was reassured that afternoon that while we may have our differences, we are also so much alike. We love each other dearly and will never lose sight of that. And, yes, I was smiling too.

⌁ PROMISE KEPT ⌁

MIDWAY INTO HIS career, Derek was asked to take a two-year assignment that required him to relocate. Divorced, his son away at college, his daughter, Suzie, fourteen and living with her mom and stepdad, he pondered the move. Believing his children were happy and comfortable in their new lives and thinking his daughter would understand his temporary absence, he accepted the new assignment.

Six months after he moved, Derek's ex-wife called and told him Suzie was beginning to act up. She was getting into trouble at school and had started smoking. Thinking about what he should do, it dawned on him that phoning his daughter to read the riot act was not the approach he should take. He was too far away to follow through on any threat of punishment he might make.

As it happens, he had given her a nickname early in her life. He always referred to her as Snoozie. It was their private term of affection, and he was the only one she permitted to use it.

Knowing how much she cherished that name, Derek decided to write Suzie a letter:

Mom tells me you are having a little trouble in school and have been smoking cigarettes. As much as it breaks my heart, I guess I have to

154

realize you are now grown up and making your own decisions. Recognizing that, I'm afraid I can no longer call you by your nickname. From now on, we'll just have to have an adult relationship.

He received a tearful phone call a few days later. Suzie was on the other end, promising him she had quit smoking and would pay attention in school, and begging him to continue to call her Snoozie.

Relieved, Derek promised his only daughter he would continue to call her by her nickname, because in his heart she would always be his little girl, no matter how old she was or what trouble she might get herself into.

Today, even though Suzie is in her midforties, Dad still calls her Snoozie, and she has kept her promises too.

"I've never stopped relying on the guidance
that only my daddy can give."

❧ FAMILY FIRST ❧

HANNAH'S FATHER LOST his job, which he had held for almost twenty-two years, during a corporate takeover. In his midfifties and with an upper-management background, he found it near impossible to secure a new job. Most of his resumes were returned with the word "overqualified" in the rejection letter. Determined anyway, he continued to send out resumes and to network every day.

There came a time when he just needed to make money to support his family, so he took what jobs he could get. He eventually found work as a stock clerk at a hardware store and a bag boy at a grocery store.

Hannah's father had always taken great pride in his executive job where he had his own office and a staff of people working for him. His new situation must be disappointing, even embarrassing for him, she thought. Yet, her dad went to work at his new jobs every day with a smile on his face. When asked how he felt about these jobs, he replied he was happy to be able to support his family. He never once complained. Instead, he made sure all knew he was proud to be making an honest living at jobs that presented their own challenges, whether they were how to keep from getting paper cuts or standing on your feet all day.

Hannah did not quite adjust to her father's change of occupation as gracefully as he did. She had enjoyed telling people about his "big important job," and now she avoided mentioning anything about the new jobs he held. Her father, however, continued to hold his head high and answered questions about his new occupation without reservation or embarrassment.

When Hannah began to support herself, even encountering a few of her own disappointments, she came to understand what her dad must have gone through, given the way his life had changed. One day she asked him how he managed to stay positive in the face of all his setbacks.

He looked at his daughter and explained it simply: no job was too small when it came to taking care of those he loved. That's when Hannah realized that his pride was never invested in the size of his desk or how many people he managed but in his family and his ability to take care of them.

Pride in family is more noble
than pride in self.

⌣ THE COMFORT OF A DAD ⌣

AFTER THE HOOPLA of Rose's fourth birthday party had passed, her dad sat her down and asked, "Do you know what a four-year-old does?" He then proceeded to tell his daughter what a four-, eight-, ten-, thirteen-, or sixteen-year-old girl does. He did this every year, telling her in his own way what was expected of a young girl or woman at that age.

The last time he gave Rose such a talk was when she turned twenty-six. Working long hours at her new job and traveling extensively, she struggled to find time to spend with her family. While having dinner with her dad and hearing of family news, she began to feel guilty about not seeing her dad as much anymore.

Dad, sensing her turmoil, put down his fork and looked across the table into her eyes. "A twenty-six-year-old is a smart, successful, and amazing businesswoman, but no matter what she accomplishes, she is always a four-year-old in her daddy's eyes."

Her dad is gone now, and each birthday Rose wishes she were four years old again, even if only for a day.

⌁HIS LITTLE CAREGIVER⁓

YEARS AGO KYLE was in a horrible accident that left him in a coma for nearly four months. His only child, Veronica, was just two years old when he became injured, but her youth didn't dissuade her desire to take care of her daddy. Every day, she sat at his feet on the hospital bed and "read" to him from her favorite picture books, all the while patting his leg and telling him that everything would be all right soon.

When Kyle emerged from the coma, it was confirmed he had suffered a severe brain injury; he had to learn to talk, walk, and care for himself all over again. Veronica was right there alongside her dad during his rehabilitation, cheering him on while he rode the stationary bicycle or lifted weights. After each physical therapy workout, she helped the nurses push his wheelchair back to his hospital room.

She also helped her dad learn to feed himself again. When food or drink spilled from his lips, Veronica wiped his mouth and reassured him with, "It's okay, Daddy, I do it too."

When Kyle was finally able to go home, Veronica helped him with his physical therapy, sometimes sitting on his feet while he did sit-ups, and with his hand exercises as he learned to switch from right- to left-hand dominance.

No one asked this little girl to help take such good care of her daddy; she just woke up each day and did it out of love.

Now sixteen years old, Veronica still helps her dad while maintaining an active academic and social life of her own. She takes him shopping or to the movies and has taught him about text messaging and online communities. Now Kyle has a new network of friends, and he and his daughter stay in constant touch with each other. She makes sure he is as involved as he can be in whatever is going on in her life.

Kyle now lives semi-independently with the support of his family. If you were to ask to see a photo of Veronica, he would quickly produce it; one is always with him. As he says, "I don't go anywhere without my little princess."

He knows, too, that he couldn't have gotten as far as he has if not for the help of his little girl, the help that was given to him purely out of love.

⌁ TIRELESS PROTECTORS ⌁

I'M SURE YOU'VE seen the television commercial featuring a dad who hugs his daughter before she leaves on a date while the boy stands at the front door. As the dad holds his daughter he looks over her shoulder and without a word but in an unmistakable expression tells the boy, "Be careful, I'm watching you."

When Ray first saw and laughed at that commercial, his twelve-year-old daughter turned to him and asked, "That's not going to be you, is it?"

Of course not, darling; what father worries about the intentions of boys who come to his door hoping to remove daddy's little girl from his immediate reach?

I told Ray of my rule about Meagan's dating. I require the young man to come inside for a chat, or the "interrogation" as Meagan calls it, so that I might determine his trustworthiness before granting him time alone with my daughter. Everyone in our house knows to stand clear of the door should I not like or be convinced by an answer given to me. As you might guess, I've already ruled out eight of ten boys from having a future as my son-in-law by the time I've asked my third or fourth question.

Ray then told me of a large wooden spoon that hangs on the wall in his daughter's bedroom. Of Italian descent, his grand-

mother and later his mother used a large wooden spoon for stir-
ring their carefully prepared sauces that simmered in large pots
on the kitchen stove. When Ray's conduct merited it, the spoon
also conveniently served its secondary purpose as a "correc-
tional instrument."

Some years after his daughter was born, he happened into
an old kitchenware store and spied on a shelf a dusty wooden
spoon. It reminded him of the one that had effectively kept him
in line as a young boy. He bought it, cleaned it up, and hung
it on the wall. When his daughter inquired why, he explained,
"When you start dating, I'm going to have a chat with every boy
that comes into this house. If I don't like his answer to any of
my questions, I'm going to whack him with that spoon."

I'm sure his daughter was no more delighted with his answer
than Meagan is in knowing what I'm going to put each prospec-
tive Romeo through on their first date, but simply put—we don't
care; it's a dad's prerogative. It's our favorite sport, making teen
boys sweat and squirm as we query them with suspicion about
their plans for the future and interest in our daughters.

My neighbor Scott, his friend, and I had lunch together recently. Scott and I have daughters; his friend has two boys. We
accused him of flirting with our waitress while she took our
orders, speculating she might now spit in the "old men's" tea
before she served it to us. He asked why we were bothered by

his flirtations, and Scott and I explained that having daughters changed the way we thought about women.

A few months ago, Scott became the proud father of his second little girl. I'm thinking about buying him a large wooden spoon, maybe two. I'm sure he'll know just what to do with them.

"Dad told me, 'Even if I lose every hair on my head in the process, I'm going to make sure you know how to take care of yourself.' And he did; I can take care of myself, thanks to him."

⌐LEAN ON ME⌐

JULIE'S DAD WAS always there for her, helping with school projects, editing papers, attending school events, being a friend when she was lonely, or helping her find her way out of unpleasant predicaments. Even now as an adult, she can still count on him to give a helping hand whenever she needs it.

As she began to plan her wedding, Julie became overwhelmed with all that had to be done. Her dad, Todd, a professional event planner, stepped in and spent hour after hour serving as her wedding planner, attending to all the details, while she enjoyed her role as the bride to be.

The wedding was a small and intimate celebration that featured carefully selected readings, prayers and music, and vows the couple had written themselves. An elegant reception followed with delicious food, libations, more music, and dancing. The day was going exactly according to plan, with one exception.

What Todd didn't plan for was the rush of emotion that overcame him as he danced with Julie at the wedding reception. As they danced, he thought back to the first time he held his daughter, just moments after she was born. Like then, tears flowed uncontrollably, and he found himself nearly speechless. Instead of the profound words he had planned to say, he could only whisper, "I love you."

It turned out to be the perfect wedding Julie had always dreamed of.

"The first time I ever saw my daddy cry was on my wedding day."

❧

✑ THINGS TREASURED ✐

DIANE'S FONDEST MEMORY of time spent with her dad is when he took her on her first boat ride on the bay. As they leaned on the railing, wind in their hair, watching the waves roll past and the sun approaching the horizon, she pointed forward and announced she had just spotted a mermaid.

Her dad laughed, scanned the horizon, and said he wished he had seen it too. Once back at the marina, he took Diane by the hand as they stepped off the boat, and together they walked to a nearby bakery. Looking into the glass case, they mulled over whether they wanted chocolate or hazelnut dessert. Unable to make up their minds, they closed their eyes and randomly pointed. With their surprise selections in hand, they sat at an outdoor table and munched on crème-filled pastries, talking until the sun finally slipped into the ocean.

Although Dad told Diane quite a few things during that evening and the many others like it that followed, he never told her there really weren't such things as mermaids. It was her youthful innocence that he treasured, and he hoped they could hold on to it just a bit longer.

↝ SHELTER FROM THE STORM ↝

TERESA IS WIRED very differently from her dad. He is laid back, simple, unassuming, and logical. Her life is demanding, time sensitive, multilayered, and filled with fast-paced activities. When she is stressed out by it all, she hits the speed dial on her office phone to call her dad.

A man of few words, "Slow down and take your time," or, "Keep your eye on the ball," might be all he'd say after answering her call and allowing her time to purge whatever was on her mind.

Even though he may not say much, in Teresa's overachieving, overscheduled life, the calming, rhythmic sound of her dad's voice is exactly what she needs to hear. It reminds her of when he patiently taught her how to fish, pitch a softball, drive the car, and play the clarinet. It also reminds her of a time when he would look at her and say, "Bundle up," or, "Get a good night's sleep." Brief statements, yes, but heartfelt expressions of a father's love and concern for his daughter nonetheless.

After each phone conversation, Teresa returns to her work calm, collected, and reassured that her dad is still her teacher, her mentor, and her safe place to run to.

❧IMITATION❧

JANET REMEMBERS SATURDAY mornings when she was a young girl, standing at her daddy's feet and waiting for him to finish making her favorite breakfast, scrambled eggs with cheese. She can still see his smile as he scooped them onto her plate and then sat down to the table with her. She could not eat those eggs fast enough, wolfing them down while they were still warm and before her dad could get up and leave to go fishing. She knew if she finished eating and was ready when he was, she would be allowed to go with him.

Janet was never left behind. Her dad planned everything around his little tomboy.

∽∶A DAD'S LASTING ROLE∶∾

AT ONE TIME or another, all children ask their parents for a bicycle. I got my own when I was about six years old, and I rode it until the sprocket literally wore out. I think I've owned three since then and rode them all just as hard, although the current one is now collecting cobwebs in a corner of our garage.

My bicycles were definitely boy toys—tall, rugged, and with all-terrain cycling gadgets attached. Meagan's first bicycle, on the other hand, was covered with girl accouterment. Painted hot pink with silver pinstripes, it had glittered starbursts scattered here and there. It had white pedals and tires, a white handlebar basket trimmed in pink, silver tassels hanging from the white handle grips, and a bell that sounded like Tinker Bell waving her magic wand. A matching pink helmet, which I purchased to protect my little girl's head, completed the ensemble.

I'd like to tell you about how quickly and effortlessly Meagan learned to ride that bike, but that wouldn't be entirely honest. Let me skip ahead a few years. One day at the beginning of summer, Meagan came to me and asked for a second bicycle, promising this time she would learn to ride it. Remembering my own fun bike riding during the summer and hoping we would finally ride bicycles together, I agreed to purchase another one for her.

Meagan surveyed the bikes in the bike shop, sat on several, and asked lots of questions before making a selection. It was a bit different from her first unused bicycle. Taller, one with a boy frame, purple but nothing frilly, it had gears but no bell. It was a bike I might have liked twenty-five years earlier.

I imagined us peddling to the bagel shop or gliding down long hills in the neighborhood with our hands held high in the air. I'd like to tell you this time she mastered the bicycle and we now ride together each weekend on the trails around our home, but that wouldn't be honest either.

I was alone when I dropped a second like-new bicycle off at the donation center.

I had forgotten about my experiences purchasing bicycles until I heard from the dad of a little girl fresh out of tricycle school.

At two and a half years old, Georgia had recently mastered riding the tricycle. In her mind, that meant she was ready to graduate to two-wheeled vehicles. Her dad agreed and then days later stayed up well into the night assembling a new bicycle for his confident little girl.

I smiled when he described the bike to me. It was painted pink with white trim, silver tassels hung from the white handle grips, and it had white tires too. It took him nearly forever to figure out how to assemble it, but he poured himself into the task, knowing he could build her first bicycle only once.

As he worked, he wondered how many "first time" experiences life would give him to share with his daughter. He thought of how quickly she was growing up and feared when he might assume she was approaching a milestone only to be informed she had already passed it and was well on her way to another one.

Somewhere in the process of turning a wrench to assemble that first bicycle, he realized growing up meant, in a way, his child would need less and less of him. He worried about losing his role of being the guy she would go to when she needed help.

I reassured him he would not lose that role in Georgia's life, but rather, what she needed from him would change. I told him of how even though Meagan has wrestled with me for independence and more than once admonished me with, "I'm not your little girl anymore," she still calls on me to take care of matters for her, some trivial, others quite difficult.

I pointed out he was certain to give Georgia driving lessons, a natural extension of bicycling, and one day he might even help her in traffic court, as I had recently done for Meagan.

Meagan never did learn to ride a bicycle, but she is leaving home for college next year. It is a milestone she has been looking forward to for years. In preparation for her departure, I am teaching her how to balance her checking account and keep up with the maintenance of her car. I hope that one day I will help her move into her first apartment, plan her wedding, and take care of her firstborn. These are only a few of the things I'm sure she'll ask me to help her with in the future.

It's going to be very difficult to watch my daughter leave home, but I know she will come back to see me. And one day, just maybe, we will be seen coasting through the neighborhood on our bicycles, our hands held high in the air.

"He brought home my first car, and my mother made him take it back because it was a sports car."

❧ MOMENTS FOR A LIFETIME ❧

OLIVIA'S PARENTS DIVORCED when she was three years old. She grew up for years without her father being a regular presence in her life. Believing he had abandoned her after the divorce, she distanced herself from him as she grew older.

Her dad, Darin, had chosen not to play a significant role in her life, mistakenly believing it best for her to be raised in one, rather than two, households. He had been raised in a divorced home and had found it confusing to live with two but separate parents who did not agree on even the most basic of things. He wanted to save his daughter that same frustration.

As time passed, however, he began to realize he did need to be a part of his daughter's life, regardless of whether he was married to her mom or not. He began to reach out, at first timidly, and eventually with willful determination.

Even though Olivia continued to push him away, he worked hard to be included in her life. His persistence began to warm her heart, and they began to build a relationship. By the time she was a teen, she began to have feelings of attachment to her father.

By the time Olivia was a wife and mother, it was known that Darin suffered from a terminal illness. He told Olivia that the pleasure of watching her succeed at her career, get married, and now have a child, was the source of his will to live. It was then that she came to believe she was important in his life after all. He might have missed the milestones of the first part of her life, but he wanted to be there for all the rest of them, he insisted, and she wanted him to be there too.

Darin began to stay in close touch with his daughter by phone or e-mail and the occasional handwritten letter. Always deeply personal, his letters touched Olivia's heart. He didn't hold anything back; he told her all the things he wished he had said when she was young. Through his writings she learned just how much she was loved by her dad.

A few years later, Olivia and her family moved to live just two doors away from her dad. One evening while sitting alone on the porch and talking about how their reunion had enhanced their lives, Olivia, then twenty-six years old, told Darin he had become the dad she could look up to and love with all her heart.

A tear rolled down his cheek as a great weight, one that had pressed against his heart for years, lifted and disappeared. He had finally heard the words he had only dreamed of until then. He no longer hoped that his daughter would forgive him and learn to love him; at that moment, he knew that she had.

ᴄ: FIRST LOVE :ᴐ

KATHERINE WALKED DOWN the aisle of the church, escorted by her father. As they reached the side of her groom to be, her father took another step forward, turned around, and stood before the couple as the pastor who would marry them.

His voice wavered as he began the ceremony, and knowing that in only a few moments he would be giving his daughter away to the new man in her life, tears came to his eyes,

As the bride watched her dad, she remembered the many times in her life when he looked after her. He simply had never let her down. There, as he stood at the front of the church and pronounced the young couple husband and wife, he was, as ever, still her love.

Every dad is his daughter's first,
and longest lasting, love.

↶ PERSISTENT LOVE ↷

LINLEY CAME INTO my life only a few years ago, so we do not have a long history together. In fact, her mother and I married around the time Linley was entering those years when she would rather be caught in a meat grinder than be seen in public having fun with an adult. I've had to be sly in my attempts to cajole her into spending time with me.

My offers to go visit the puppies at a nearby pet store or take her to get a manicure or an ice cream often result in her consent to go on an "outing." When all else fails, I offer a meal at the Chinese restaurant of her choice. It is a sure bet; she always jumps at the chance to eat wonton soup and house lo mein.

In between listening to her laugh at the fact I was born in the year of the rat, watching as she picks wontons out of her soup and vegetables out of her lo mein, and seeing the juice of the dessert oranges run down her arms, we talk about school and the things of concern to youth her age. Along the way, I gain a little more insight into what makes her tick. When she tires of my parental queries, she deftly changes the subject to giving me advice on which habits I should break and which I should develop. With her help, it seems, I could become a little less boring.

As I listen, I remember when Meagan was her age, just as blissfully naive and optimistic and needing real-life experiences to buttress her youthful confidence. In such moments, I ponder the role I play in Linley's life as her stepdad. I think of all the things I want to teach her, warn her about, and make sure she is able to handle before she, too, sets out on her own one day. Preparing her for independence is a job I share with her mother and father, and I pray that between us all she receives the guidance she needs to conquer what challenges may one day be thrown in her path.

As we finish our meals and head home, she thanks me for the time we've spent together. I smile and begin to plan the next time I will ask her to go on an outing with me. Hopefully, before she leaves home, she will let me call our little excursions for what they are to me—dates.

Dads fear letting their daughters down.
Daughters seldom think they do.

❖ WORDS OF COMFORT ❖

FRANK WAS A MAILMAN for over forty years. He had a walking route through a neighborhood near his home, and most of the residents on his route knew him by name. They also knew his little sidekick, his daughter, Patty, whom he sometimes called Dolly Dimple. She accompanied him as he delivered mail during the summer and on Saturdays and never complained about rising early to go to work. It was, after all, her idea. She jumped at the chance to ring the doorbell when there was a package or bundle of magazines to deliver. She loved spending time alone with and helping her dad.

One day while on his route, Frank began to hum a song. Patty recognized it immediately. Within moments they were singing the Mickey Mouse Club theme song at the top of their lungs. After that day, it became part of their daily routine. Whenever he noticed Patty was sad, not feeling well, or just needing a laugh, he promptly began to sing the song. It always put a smile back on her face.

When the day of her wedding arrived, Patty stood waiting for her cue to begin her walk down the aisle toward her future husband. Frank looked over and saw how nervous she was. He squeezed her hand, winked, and began to softly sing their favorite song. The happy bride's jitters drained away, and she laughed all the way down the aisle. She barely remembers hearing the wedding march, entranced by the soothing voice singing what was by then more than just a playful song. It was a symbol of their enduring bond.

As Patty's life became full with her growing family, she saw less of her dad, and he found fewer opportunities to sing to her. Although their bond remained as strong as ever, their lives had diverged. Their song was replaced with discussions about raising children, aging, and other challenges of daily living. That, too, would change, and abruptly.

Shortly after celebrating her parents' fifty-second wedding anniversary, Patty sat dumbstruck as her father, a lifelong non-smoker, announced to his family that he had inoperable lung cancer. She couldn't believe her ears when she heard he had only a few months to live. Tears suddenly flooded her cheeks.

To ease the shock as the bad news sank in, Frank began to sing the Mickey Mouse song for all. His voice was wispy and weak but magical nonetheless. Patty couldn't help herself—she began to smile through her tears.

Putting her other responsibilities aside, she began to accompany her dad to each of his medical appointments. During those times, they reflected on their life together, especially all those days walking through the neighborhood, back when he occasionally let her slide the mail into the mailboxes.

During some of those appointments, particularly when news from the doctor was worse than discouraging, Patty quietly sang the same comforting song to her father in the way that he had sung to her on so many occasions before. This time, it was Frank who began to smile through his tears.

One afternoon, knowing her days left with her dad were limited, Patty asked him to sing along with her into a tape recorder. Realizing she wanted something special to remember him with, he agreed and then sang better than he had for a long time.

Now, when she misses him more than she can bear, Patty listens to that recording. As it always has, their favorite song still puts a smile on her face.

∾A LEGACY OF LOVE∾

I REMEMBER ATTENDING an awards program one evening at Meagan's day care when she was four years old. I can still see her, all of forty inches tall, wearing a white cap and gown, with white sandals, and her little fingernails and toenails painted pale pink. She stood in line with her friends, rising up on her tiptoes several times in an effort to find me in the crowd. I jockeyed for position with the other parents who were also trying to get in the right spot for a perfect photograph of their child. She spied me, waved, and pointed me out to the girl standing next to her. I grinned, waved back, and quickly took several photos.

The moment for giving out the awards arrived. The day-care director gave a brief speech about cherishing the memories of these formative years and then offered each child a piece of paper rolled up like a diploma. When Meagan's turn came, she received a certificate for being the most talkative (it was well deserved). Everyone laughed, she blushed, and soon the ceremony was over. Afterward, we were served Kool-Aid and Oreos, and I took more photos of Meagan, this time while she hammed it up with several of her young friends.

I was known to her friends back then as "Meagan's dad." I loved that name because it was such a pure and simple description of who I was. The kids don't know of my accomplishments and failures. I was just Meagan's dad, the silly guy who made them laugh in the afternoons and occasionally got down on the floor alongside his daughter during nap time before leaving town on a business trip.

One of the things I enjoyed most in those years was the untarnished innocence of their young age. Judgment, embarrassment, and expectation had not yet entered their lives. In Meagan's eyes, I was simply the guy who let her ride on my shoulders, the man who let her eat spaghetti with her fingers, the father who helped her get ready for bed, and the daddy who read a nighttime story to her, using a different voice for each character. If I disappointed her back then, she's forgotten about it. Thankfully, today her memories of childhood nearly always bring forth hearty laughter.

But I know I've disappointed Meagan many times since her kindergarten years, and I do worry that I've done some things she won't forget. Often after my teenager and I have had an argument or simply just can't seem to get along, my heart sinks as I try to convince myself I'm not a failure as a parent.

It is during those moments of doubt when I pull a photo out of my wallet, one taken the evening of that awards ceremony long ago. I've carried it with me every day in the last dozen-plus years. The look in Meagan's eyes still stirs me. The smile on her face reminds me of a promise I made in the first moment I held her after she was born: to be the best father I could be. In the end, only Meagan can say if I've lived up to that promise, but in the interim, I find some measure of satisfaction knowing that at least I *tried* to be a good dad.

This book will probably begin to appear in stores about the time Meagan, my inspiration for becoming an author in the first place, turns eighteen and makes her final preparations to leave home. As she begins her new life out from under my wing, I hope she will reflect back on her time with me and decide for herself that she was and still wants to be daddy's little girl. If she does, I think that will be the best reward I can ask for.

It will mean I have been a good dad after all.

❧ SHARE YOUR FAVORITE MEMORY ❧

_____

_____

_____

_____

_____

_____

_____

_____

_____

_____

_____

_____

_____

_____

↧ ACKNOWLEDGMENTS ↦

The writing of *Daddy's Little Girl: Stories of the Special Bond Between Fathers and Daughters* has been a journey of labor, love, and discovery, a journey that I could not have experienced without the generous support and encouragement of many people. I would like to give a heartfelt thanks to the following:

My wife, Jill, who did more than her fair share of chores around our home and for our family during the months that I worked on this project, who listened to me whine, and who did not shame me for my forgetfulness and occasional irritability. I love her beyond measure; she is my best friend. I must also thank her for her tireless efforts editing my final draft, although I do think she went a little overboard deleting my semicolons; I rather liked them.

My daughter, Meagan, the inspiration for most of what I write. Thank you, darlin', for being so willing (or at least tolerant), allowing me to document our relationship in such a public manner. I hope that as the years go by, you will see in my written words more and more of my undivided love for you.

My step-daughter, Linley, the new addition to my heart and home, who reminds me everyday that parenting is a challenge, a joy, a celebration, and sometimes, a unique blend of improvisation and stand-up comedy.

My editor, Cynthia DiTiberio, who patiently guided me through the development, rewrites, and finishing touches of this book, who was kind each time she said, "try again," and who continues to encourage me. Cynthia, I look forward to working on our next book together.

My agent, Andrew Stuart, who found me and took me to the proverbial next level, worked with me to develop the right idea, and then stayed faithful to his promises throughout the search to find a home for this book. Thank you, Andrew, for opening new doors for me.

My family, friends, and neighbors who stayed patient with me as I posed, reposed, and posed them again in a vain effort to capture the perfect photographs to illustrate this book. Thank you all for being the faces to accompany my words.

I also wish to thank all the fathers and daughters who told me heartwarming, poignant, and sometimes difficult stories about their daddy-daughter relationship. Without their willingness to share the details of their lives, this book could not have been written. Every story told to me did not make it into this book, but every story helped me tremendously in each word I wrote. Furthermore, my life is richer now because of the relationships I've made with those who so generously and patiently dealt with me probing into their lives. I hope to take you all up on your offers to stop by for dinner. And if you are ever in Duluth, please have a seat on the porch with me. I'm sure there is plenty we could talk about.

❧ TELL ME YOUR STORIES ❧

People in all times and places have told stories. Stories have probably been shared in every family in every culture as a means of entertainment and preservation of family history, and to instill knowledge, wisdom, and moral values in youth. Traditionally, family stories were passed from generation to generation in the car during road trips, in a rocking chair on the porch, around the dinner table, at family reunions, weddings or funerals, and whenever the need arose to help someone better understand a significant life event or challenge. Such stories are often lessons that still teach even though generations may have passed since the events of the story originally unfolded.

Family stories also all too often survive only in memory, and as such, slowly fade away. I would like to capture important family stories while they are still fresh in the hearts and minds of those who tell them. I want to give longevity to stories about family, love, and faith that can inspire others for years, even generations, to come.

If you have an inspirational story to share, one you think others will enjoy and perhaps learn an important life lesson from, please tell it to me.

Submit your stories to:

Gregory E. Lang
3455 Peachtree Industrial Blvd.
Suite 305–306
Duluth, GA 30096

or over the Internet at www.gregoryelang.com

To contact the author, e-mail greg.lang@mindspring.com.

"The first time I laid eyes on her,
I saw my greatest dream come true.
I had me a little girl."

❧

❧ ❧ ❧